What people are saying about

A Guide to Pilgrimage

If you have ever felt curious about the act of pilgrimage, or are already a seasoned traveller in search of the sacred, Thea's book offers much to enjoy. With a fascinating historical overview, personal experiences, and useful advice and tools to plan and execute your own quest, *A Guide to Pilgrimage* will inspire you to take those first magical steps on your spiritual odyssey.
Eimear Burke, Storyteller and Chosen Chief of the Order of Bards, Ovates and Druids

This is a beautiful book, full of soulfulness and an innate sense of the sacred. Thea's *A Guide to Pilgrimage* is both accessible and deeply wise in its exploration of the vast and important subject. Packed with historical information as well as practical advice and insights for the modern pilgrim, this is a delight to read and sure companion along the way.
Danú Forest, (MA Celtic Studies) traditional wisewoman, writer and teacher. Author of *Wild Magic - Celtic Folk Traditions for the Solitary Practitioner*

A Guide to Pilgrimage by Thea Prothero is a concise and insightful introduction to this ancient tradition. She documents her own pilgrimage to Iona as well as interviewing pilgrims from different faiths. The structured steps Prothero outlines will help potential pilgrims make the most of their journeys, and the additional hints and tips throughout the volume will enrich their experience. This book is an invaluable guide to all those who want to take a step outside of the mundane world.
Andrew Anderson, author of *Ritual of Writing, Artio & Artaois* and *The Magic of Cats*

Thea takes the deep connection and spiritual journey of the Pilgrimage and makes it accessible for those on alternative spiritual paths. Through sharing her inspirational personal experiences, she leads the reader towards their own growth and self-discovery. *A Guide to Pilgrimage* is a thought provoking and uplifting book from which Thea's knowledge and passion for the subject shines through.

Katie Gerrad, author of *Odin's Gateways* and *Seidr: The Gate Is Open*

Thea Prothero's book, *A Guide to Pilgrimage,* is a call to action and adventure. With instructions for preparation and stories of pilgrimages across traditions, readers will not only be inspired but will also get a map to guide them from the smallest whisper of desire to the actual physical steps at the sites. This book encouraged me to take the next steps for pilgrimages I have always wanted to take, and I'm grateful for the push from this book.

Irisanya Moon, author of *Artemis - Goddess of the Wild Hunt & Sovereign Heart* and *Gaia: Saving Her, Saving Ourselves*

A Guide to Pilgrimage contains everything you need to discover, plan and undertake your own journey. From definitions to historical facts, through modern day examples and personal experiences author, Thea Prothero, has got pilgrimage covered. This beautiful book is full of (non-denominational) faith and spirit, including the author's generous sharing of her own vision and 'miracle'. Inspirational and highly recommended reading.

June Kent, Editor of *Indie Shaman* magazine

If you have ever been drawn to a place that has refused to leave your thoughts, then this practical guide is for you. *A Guide to Pilgrimage,* by Thea Prothero is a book that will be of use on your journey to historical locations in the UK and abroad. This delightful guide explores the history of the pilgrim's journey from different perspectives and cultures through the ages. Pilgrimage is a compelling and intriguing read, with Thea visiting pagan and Christian sites as an escape from the busy modern world on her quest for meaning and understanding. She encourages the reader to absorb and connect with each place visited with devotional practices, meditation and reflection afterwards. It is a helpful, passionate guide for finding your pilgrimage path in the 21st Century.

Scott Irvine, author of *The Magic of Serpents*, and *Ishtar & Ereshkigal*

Pagan Portals
A Guide to Pilgrimage

Pagan Portals
A Guide to Pilgrimage

Thea Prothero

MOON BOOKS

London, UK
Washington, DC, USA

CollectiveInk

First published by Moon Books, 2024
Moon Books is an imprint of Collective Ink Ltd.,
Unit 11, Shepperton House, 89 Shepperton Road, London, N1 3DF
office@collectiveinkbooks.com
www.collectiveinkbooks.com
www.moon-books.net

For distributor details and how to order please visit the 'Ordering' section on our website.

Text copyright: Thea Prothero 2023

ISBN: 978 1 80341 686 1
978 1 80341 687 8 (ebook)
Library of Congress Control Number: 2023947377

A CIP catalogue record for this book is available from the British Library.

Design: Lapiz Digital Services

UK: Printed and bound by CPI Group (UK) Ltd, Croydon, CR0 4YY
Printed in North America by CPI GPS partners

We operate a distinctive and ethical publishing philosophy in all areas of our business, from our global network of authors to production and worldwide distribution.

CONTENTS

Introduction

Have you ever felt drawn to a place, somewhere you have not visited? Maybe you have come across a picture online, or seen this particular place in a film or read about it in a magazine and something resonates inside you? Do you feel a deep need to find out more, or maybe even go there? The place might not be a usual holiday destination or look easy to get to – but even when you find all the excuses not to consider going there – the place refuses to leave your thoughts. Eventually when you think you have forgotten all about it, something small and trivial will remind you...

Let me tell you, you are definitely not alone. As a teenager, I kept having a reoccurring dream about a small island surrounded with sapphire blue seas. On the island was a small rustic chapel, and along a single track which meandered along the length of the island, there stood a huge stone cross richly decorated and patterned and that was much taller than me. I found a smooth green stone which sat beautifully in my hand, so comfortably, that I hadn't been aware of it. I placed at the foot of the cross. The dream was so realistic that I could smell the salt in the air from the sea, I was warmed by the sunshine and the breeze in my hair and feel the smooth texture of the stone in my hand. This was a real puzzle to me as a young person, especially as I am not a Christian and I had never visited such an island in my life.

After a time, when the mystery behind this dream didn't become clearer, I assumed it was a strange fiction, and put it completely out of my mind and got on with my life. That is, until decades later when by chance I was watching an episode of the BBC programme *Sacred Wonders of Britain*. The presenter, Neil Oliver, was on a small boat in the Inner Hebrides on the coast of Scotland and as the camera panned around from him, it showed an island surrounded by sapphire seas with a church-like building in the distance – I felt something deep inside me shift...like an imprint of a memory so profoundly powerful that as I watched in awe as I saw not only the tall cross that I had dreamed about long ago, but a beach famous for its particular type of green stone...Iona.

From that moment I knew not only that I would go there myself one day, but strangely, that it had to be at the right time. I then sought as much information as I could find about the island, and I even had a necklace with a piece of Iona Green stone set in it! Does this ring any bells with you?

Perhaps you are still seeking your place but have felt a yearning that you want to change something inside you or searching a new way of thinking or being in the world. Did you yearn to step away from the modern life and spend some time in nature? Maybe you have toyed with the idea of a pilgrimage but are unsure what exactly it is and how it would fit in with your busy life?

If so, then I am hoping this book will be of use to you in your quest. I have tried to make this body of work a practical guide to finding your pilgrimage path, whether you follow a religious or spiritual way or just want to make sense of your need to do a pilgrimage, or not.

In this book you will find my stories of pilgrimage, an overview on the history of this very ancient practice and illustrations of different faiths who observe pilgrimage as part of their spiritual devotions. Here you will find experiences of pilgrimage from different perspectives, different tools – meditations, and journaling, for example, to enable you to understand and create your own unique quest.

So, what is a pilgrimage?

Simply put, a pilgrimage is a journey to a specific destination. This destination is usually somewhere of meaning, such as a place of spiritual or religious significance, or a site associated with an important or meaningful event, or of importance to the pilgrim. There are dozens of reasons people go on a pilgrimage; to seek meaning in their lives, to deepen their relationship with their belief system, or the hope of achieving personal transformation. It may simply be to step away from their everyday lives and to spend time in nature, away from technology and to get fitter.

Most pilgrimages are linear, that is to say they start at one place and arrive at a different place, and involve a journey spread over a number of days, weeks, or months, depending on how the journey is travelled and what the goal of the pilgrimage is. Often the journey is through a landscape, culture, or country unknown to the pilgrim, adding to the experience of separation from the everyday reality of their lives.

When eventually the pilgrimage reaches the final destination, time is typically spent absorbing and connecting with the place, including devotional practices, meditation or preforming a traditional act of faith, or whatever the goal was for the pilgrim in reaching this place.

Finally, the pilgrim returns to their everyday lives, family, job, and home. Time may be needed to reflect and come to terms with the whole experience, undoubtedly the person will be changed in lots of ways, and this can take time to fully process before fully integrating back into their old life. You will be renewed, fitter and have more purpose than ever before.

Chapter 1

The History of Pilgrimage

Historically, pilgrimages have taken place for over three thousand years in one form or another as a devotional practice. It may surprise you to discover that, to ancient civilisations, pilgrimage was an observance that everyday people took part in and was an important function of their spiritual traditions. Ancient Egyptians, for example, would travel to Abydos, west of the river Nile in pilgrimage to honour the god Osiris, their dearest wish was to eventually be buried there, or as near to as they could afford. The importance of this was encouraged and supported by the successive Pharaohs who enlarged and embellished the temple of Osiris with opulent riches.

In ancient Greece, the consultation of the Oracles meant that people travelled over huge distances to Delphi, which the god Zeus considered to be the navel of Gaia (mother earth) although earlier myths suggest that the Pythia was a well-established oracle and high priestess of the temple of Apollo, prior to this. The Pythia was one of the most powerful women of the Ancient Greeks, her prestige and prophecies were highly sought after. At the Temple of Zeus in Dodona was another oracle who attracted pilgrims from far beyond the Greek borders, destroyed and re-built by the Roman emperor Augustus, the oracle was consulted by the Emperor Julian in 362 before his campaign against the Persians. The oracle was still sought by pilgrims until 392 when the Christian Emperor Theodosius closed all pagan religious sites down.

During the Middle Ages in Europe, Christian pilgrimage became a significant occupation for everyone who had the ability to do it. It became fashionable for Kings and Royals to make pilgrimage to Rome, the seat of the Holy Roman empire.

In 853 the young Alfred (later known as The Great,) went to visit his holiness the Pope with his father, King Aethelwulf. In later years, Alfred believed his confirmation and being made Council of Rome, (a spiritual son of the pope was a pinnacle in his becoming King of England. In 1027, King Cnut was possibly the last English monarch to make this journey, and the first Christian of Viking decent to gain audience with the pope.

Not all so-called pilgrimages during the Middle Ages were peaceful or even what we would define a pilgrimage today. Between 1095 and 1291 a series of wars occurred directed by the Latin church. Known as the Crusades, the wars against the Muslim Empire were made to regain the lands surrounding Jerusalem, the place of Jesus Christs death and burial, known as the Holy Lands. The Church promised knights who took part in the Crusades, forgiveness of their sins, amongst other rewards, for going to war. The first Crusade was actually called a *peregrinatio* – which translates as pilgrimage. After a long siege, Jerusalem was captured in 1099 with thousands killed. However, by the end in 1291, the Crusaders had not managed to hold on to any of lands the Church sought.

Pilgrimage wasn't just for the rich and famous. In the middle ages, over one fifth of the European population had a direct connection to pilgrimage, either by going on one, or having a links to the sites. The common people believed that by going on a pilgrimage to visit a sacred shrine, which was supposed to house a relic (a tooth, finger, or blood, for example) from a saint or other holy person, or a holy well or sacred waters for healing, would ensure their place in Heaven, that they would be cured or a range of ailments and they would be forgiven all their sins. This is the time when the famous pilgrim routes and places came into prominence. The most popular in England was to the shrine of Thomas Beckett at Canterbury Cathedral. Indeed, Geoffrey Chaucer's most famous work *The Canterbury Tales* was written at this time, depicting a set of tales by a group of pilgrims travelling to Canterbury together to visit the Beckett's shrine. At this time, most people who undertook pilgrimage walked for months to reach the final destination. The road was hard and dangerous, people travelled in groups for protection against criminals. Pilgrims would sometimes be forced to sleep by the roadside in all weathers and rely on the kindness of strangers for food. This abstinence from physical comforts would, however, bring you into a state of grace in the eyes of God.

Another famous pilgrim site in the UK is Walsingham, in Norfolk. The original pilgrimage site was founded in 1061, when the lady of the manor had a vision of the Virgin Mary and Angel Gabriel. She was instructed to build a replica of the Holy House in Nazareth at Walsingham. This then became a centre of pilgrimage and in the 12th century a priory was built to protect the Holy House and offer pilgrims sanctuary whilst visiting. The last mile, from the aptly named slipper chapel, to the shrine, was often walked bare foot. The slipper chapel is today the Roman Catholic Shrine. During the Dissolution of the monasteries, in 1536, the priory and holy buildings were destroyed, and the wooden Holy House was raised to the ground.

A new shrine was erected in the 1930's in a new Holy House

and pilgrims were encouraged to return to Walsingham again. A Saxon well was discovered during the laying of the foundations. This is believed to be the holy well where medieval pilgrims would go for healing.

During late 2022 I visited Walsingham to experience this Christian place of pilgrimage for myself. The village, which in itself feels like it has been frozen in time, seems to have no less than three spiritual centres. The first is the beautifully recreated Holy House in the Anglican Shrine of Our lady, which includes relics from the cross and the afore mentioned Holy well. This has all been sympathetically recreated to appear as authentic as possible. On entering the shrine, the sense of serenity is overpowering. Everyone walks around with hushed voices, and light candles at the various chapels dotted about. Everybody is made to feel welcome, and encouraged to spend as much, or as little time as they like in each area. The sense of peace and history of devotion is so strong that I found sitting in the Holy House among others deep in prayer, overwhelming. The grounds of the Shrine are an elegant garden reminiscent of the Chalice Well in Glastonbury. On the day of my visit, a sunny autumnal day, the gardens were full of tourists and the devoted alike. Children enjoyed running along the paths and several people were sitting on the grass. It was, in comparison to the Shrine, much more relaxed.

On leaving the Shrine and its grounds, I visited the original site of the Priory and the Holy House, which is very nearby. This is now more of a formal park, with a very poignant tiny marker in the ground where the original Holy House once stood. All that remains of the Priory is the ruins, most notable is the East Window Arch, I tried to imagine how magnificent it must have been with strained glass. The grounds have a feeling of a graveyard in their emptiness. To the side of the gardens is a crypt, which is the only remaining room from the priory left.

Just outside the actual town is the Roman catholic shrine, which is unfortunately closed at the time I visited. However, although it is small in comparison to the other sites, has an important role in catholic pilgrimage to this day. On returning home, I watched the video on the website, called The Walsingham Way, which gave me more insight into the area and belief within this Shrine.

I often visit churches, cathedrals, and holy places. Although I am not of the Christian faith, I appreciate the power of devotion in such locations. The layering of history from communal belief is one of the most commanding feelings I have ever experienced. Visiting this place of Christian pilgrimage gave me a sense of the impressive history of the faith in my country. Although I don't share the beliefs, I do appreciate the dedication and love which is poured into this sacred site.

Returning to the history of pilgrimage, it was sometimes used as penance for a sin or crime, of varying degrees of seriousness, which often lead to disapproval from members of the church, and result in obvious dangers to others. For example, someone found guilty of acts of violence is sent unaccompanied on a long journey, it's not hard to imagine what might have happened!

For economic reasons, pilgrimage became a vital source of money for churches and even the towns surrounding them. Commerce in souvenirs and symbols of pilgrimage, which every pilgrim would, of course, covet and purchase as a sign of the completion of their pilgrimage, became common place. Tens of thousands of pilgrim badges have been found since the 19th century mainly in rivers, they are the most common pieces of art found from the Middle Ages. The trade in Pilgrim badges, which at the time, could be purchased everywhere around each place of veneration, and bore specific imagery relating to the site, was widespread and were affordable to everyone. Often made of lead and mass produced, they were affixed with a pin on the back and worn on outer clothing. At the height of the Middle Ages, popular sites of veneration would sell over 100,000 a year. Another common souvenir was an ampullae, a small vial filled with water from the well or holy site and worn around the neck. The most recognised symbol, still used today, is the scallop shell which represents the Camino di Santiago pilgrim route or Way of St James.

The cult of Christian pilgrimage in the UK began to lessen significantly between the 15th and 16th centuries. With the dissolution of the monasteries by Henry VIII, sites of veneration and elaborately decorated reliquaries housing holy relics were largely destroyed or taken into private collections. The new Protestant religion used simpler iconography in its churches, and the frivolity of pilgrimage was frowned upon. Emphasis was instead placed upon the individual's internal journey to grace. By 1536 the shrine of Thomas a Beckett was destroyed, and the bishop of St David's cathedral ordered pilgrimage to cease.

The years of 1536-7 were significant as it was the time of widespread revolt against Henry VIII and his separation from Rome in the north of England. Known as the *Pilgrimage of Grace.* This was a series of rebellions which became a serious threat to the government of the time. At its height, 40,000 men were involved across Lincolnshire and Yorkshire, led by Robert Aske, who was a skilled speaker and zealous Catholic, and came up with the title *Pilgrimage of Grace,* linking up with the idea of returning the church to Rome. As the rebellion grew in strength, and began to spread south, Henry used delaying tactics and insisted the leaders come to London to answer questions, whereupon they were arrested and tried for treason. Aske was taken back to Yorkshire where he was executed.

There was a resurgence of small-scale pilgrimage in the late 18th and19th centuries with the rise of the Romantic and Neogothic movements. Travel was only for the wealthy and travel companies specialising in trips to Rome and the Holy lands, began to offer specialised package holidays to the well-to-do tourists and adventurers. The Grand Tour was already an established rite of passage, and became more widely available with the railways from the 1840's. While not strictly pilgrimage in the original sense, the possibility and ease of travel meant that old pilgrim sites had new visitors. Around this time a 14-year-old girl saw a vision of the Virgin Mary near Lourdes, which lead to new sites of pilgrimage being established.

This leads us nicely to the next chapter on Pilgrimage in the modern day.

Chapter 2

Modern Day Pilgrimage

Stepping forward into the present day, pilgrimage is still widely recognised in its more traditional form relating to a religious quest. For example, every year 30,000 pilgrims climb Croagh Patrick in Co. Mayo Ireland on the last Sunday of July, known as Reek Sunday. Many climb bare footed or even on their knees, as it is considered an act of penance in the Catholic Church.

Over 347,000 people completed the Camino de Santiago in 2019, breaking all previous records. The Camino is the most famous group of pilgrimage routes in the world. The symbol of the Camino de Santiago is the scallop shell which has in modern times become the symbol for pilgrimage in general. The Camino De Santiago, or Way of St. James in English, is a network of pilgrim ways leading to the Cathedral of Santiago de Compostela in Galicia, Northern Spain. This is the shrine of the apostle St. James who is supposedly buried here after relics were found in the ninth century.

There are at least six well established ways, the most popular is Camino Frances which, starts in St John Pied de Port, France, and takes on average 25 days or more and is 772 km in length. This being the most popular route, means in the summer it gets quite busy and lodgings along the way tend to get booked up. Today, over 220,000 people walk or cycle the Camino annually, with differing spiritual beliefs, or none, and from all over the world. The Camino is actively promoted as a tourist activity by the local Galician government, meaning the figures have been rising steadily.

Amanda Kilroy is a shamanic teacher and wild leader who lives near Dartmoor. She shared her experience of following the Camino Frances with me:

I did this in 2010, which I remember was a "holy year". I did it in Sept/Oct because of the heat! I went from St Jean Pied de Port and went on past Santiago to Finisterre – which was the completion point for the pagan route that predates the Christian journey. I travelled alone – although I met so many people and walked with some people for a few days at a time.

Why did you decide to do it?

There wasn't one reason. It had been in my awareness for some time – because of books I'd read – Shirley MacLaine's, "Camino" and The Pilgrimage by Paulo Coelho. And then a friend of mine did the walk, and he gave me the shell he had carried, so I kind of felt that a baton had been handed to me. But also, my children were grown – I was a very young mum – two daughters by the age of 26 – so it felt like I wanted to do something on my own. It felt like a bit of a rite of passage, from motherhood to what might come next. I remember I used to talk about wanting to just move out into the world, navigating from my belly – not being on a schedule, taking and picking anyone up from school. I wanted to drop into a deeper flow, another rhythm. It was so weird when I saw the first shell (the sign that guides you as you walk). I welled up. It was like being a pearl in a string that stretched across time. I remember the sense of that vividly. Like joining a stream of people seeking not a destination, but a stream or flow towards something – spiritually significant.

What did you get out of it?

That's another huge question. At the time I guess I drew strength and direction from it. It was one of the most profound tests of my life. To set off alone, not knowing the way, if it was safe, or how to do anything. Trusting the process of walking. It felt like a form of wilding – unhooking from life's routine and testing my own limits. Physically it was hard. My body struggled. I didn't have the right shoes for the weather. My feet had perpetual blisters, my shoulders hurt, and my periods stopped, because I was walking every day – from 21 to 44k – which was my longest distance. I walked almost every day for six weeks. It was intense. Sometimes I was aware of the physicality and the strain. Other times that wasn't a factor at all. People said when I left to do it – "are you going to find yourself" and what I said to them after was this, it was the most profound experience of emptying, of losing myself if anything – that was what I found. Time would go by when I was so completely absorbed that thoughts would evaporate, leaving an emptiness and space – a hum in my body of being that was truly delicious. I loved how it made me feel so grounded, rooted, part of the earth. I remember walking through the Pyrenees, and marvelling. I remember walking for a whole day, up a steep incline in pouring rain, and then emerging above the clouds, and seeing the way before me as part of the heavens. Weeping for the sheer majesty of that experience. That was the closest I've ever felt to God. The churches were impressive, but they did nothing for me. It was the different hues of each dawn. Being present for the turning of the season. Cooking in the evenings with people of all nationalities. Being so utterly spent that I could drop my clothes in a dormitory and jump straight into bed – not caring about the infamous bed bugs, or who might be watching. Being– in flow – alone – with others – deeply myself. I draw upon all my experiences from that time even now. It is part of me. It still forges me.

How did you feel when you got back?

Really strange and a bit dislocated. I stayed connected with people I met on the road, because only they understood. There was an acute awareness of the speed of normal life – the insanity. I didn't want to go back into it – and I didn't – It was six months before I went back to work again. I just couldn't let go of the feeling of being, the camaraderie, the proximity to nature, to spirit, and to myself. I remember walking everywhere for a while. Needing to stay connected. I remember feeling like I'd really changed, but everything and everyone else was still the same.

Did it change you?

One big change that happened was that I developed boundaries. Before I did that walk, I occupied this role in our family. I was always the one that people called. The one who dropped everything to support my mum and sister – or anyone else. When I came back, I started saying no to things. I saw how people fed off my energy and didn't respect my path. This is something that has continued.

Would you recommend it?

Yes, and often do! I've also continued walking. I get outside, in a particular attitude of walking. I do this when I need to process something or reconnect. I do it when I'm writing or creating. There's a rhythm and presence which only happens when you are walking.

Maybe you are wondering, how can pilgrimage relate to me? Our modern lives are busy, moving at a fast pace, sometimes chaotically, and technology only heightens our impatience for everything. Now. Collectively, our religious beliefs have generally waned, and been replaced with other more earthly and human centred concerns. How many of you remember the scenes in *Forrest Gump* where he *"Just decided to go for a little run"*? In the film, the title character, played by Tom Hanks, started running and didn't stop until he's crossed the USA several times. In one scene he is pursued by reporters who ask him, "*Are you doing this for world peace? Are you doing this for the homeless...*" I expect you have seen adverts by charities asking people to do a sponsored event, walking a certain number of miles, or between certain points raising money for a good cause, or maybe you have taken part. Although the end result is monetary, there is a specific aim – helping others, less fortunate, which could be construed as worthy and soul fulfilling in the same way pilgrims achieve their religious goals when completing a pilgrimage.

The idea of walking (or running) to make the world a better place, or a healthier one, largely started in the USA in 1953 with a woman, known as the Peace Pilgrim. She vowed to continue walking all over the USA and Mexico until there was peace in the world and kept going for twenty-eight years! With only the clothes she wore, relying on the kindness of strangers and spreading the ideals of a better world through peace, she transferred the belief that seeking a better place in heaven was something only a god could grant, by setting a human example and thus making real political change. In 1963 a crowd of over 250,000 walked between the Washington Monument and Lincoln Memorial in Washington D.C on the March for Jobs and Freedom to see Martin Luther King give his famous "I have a Dream" speech. In the UK 'Hunger Marches' had begun in the 1920's as a reaction to high levels of unemployment and poverty after World War 1. The most prominent happened in 1936, when 200 men marched from Jarrow in County Durham to Parliament in protest against unemployment and poverty in the Tyneside area of the UK. The three-hundred-mile route taken by the men took nearly a month, and included stops at Ripon and Northampton where they were fed and housed. The petition handed in to Parliament ensured that working conditions and social reform improved after the Second World War.

In 2016 Elvis Presley's mansion, Graceland, which opened to the public in 1982, marked its twenty million visitors. You may be wondering why I have added this information in a book on pilgrimage. Let's look at the facts: Every year the estate hosts an Elvis Week, regularly attended by over 10,000 people and which coincides with the day Elvis died (August 15th) when they have an All Night Vigil. Fans line up, for hours and days on end, to make offerings and lay flowers at 'The King's' grave. Doesn't this have very striking similarities to visiting a religious shrine? Especially so at the height of pilgrimage when pilgrims would queue for hours to pay their respects, and possibly leave offerings to the saint. For Elvis fans, this veneration at the graveside, during the all-night vigil, is the culmination of their pilgrimage to Graceland. For his devoted fans, this is a special journey that costs a lot of money and requires careful planning and can be physically demanding. The offerings themselves sometimes include pleas for Elvis to intervene with God or have a confessional element.

Modern day pilgrimages to graves and significant places relating to famous people, is one of the most popular forms pilgrimage has taken in contemporary society. I for one have done this. In 2008, as a final year student studying photography, I made a pilgrimage to Heptonstall in West Yorkshire to visit the grave of the poet Sylvia Plath. I had been using her poems to create a set of self-portraits and wanted to pay my respects and lay flowers on her grave. The journey to Heptonstall wasn't an easy one. I had my camera/tripod and other equipment with me, and it was February with the threat of snow, as I climbed the steep hill on the Calderdale way. I felt as though I had stepped into Ted Hughes (Sylvia Path's husband) world of whirling winds and remote otherworldly wildness. I made my way through the ethereal churchyard and ruined church dating from 1260, (made even more ethereal, by the swirling sleet that surrounded me,) to the more modern cemetery. It was a true awakening, and I felt a strong connection to both of them. When faced with the grave, I was overcome with emotion, having reached the end, both of Plath and my work on that project. I laid bedraggled tulips and muttered a few words of thanks. The feeling of completion and strength I drew from that pilgrimage enabled me to finish my degree and look beyond the physical in every part of my own creativity.

You may have done something similar to this, without even considering it relevant to pilgrimage? Have you ever visited a place of personal significance, a famous battle ground or a celebrity's memorial site, for example?

Returning to a more traditional form of pilgrimage, its transcendent nature sits very well with modern and New Age spirituality. There has been a resurgence of those travelling to historical pilgrimage sites, such as Glastonbury, along with other sites of pre-historic interest, like Orkney or Stonehenge and natural beauty spots; all places where the veil between the mundane and the Otherworld is thin, making the spiritual vibes more pronounced and available. These remarkable places offer a chance of spiritual enlightenment and personal growth.

Going back a step to what I said earlier, our modern lives are full-up with time consuming commitments, work, and family, not to mention the costs involved which often have to take precedence over spiritual growth. People in general just can't take the time to go off on pilgrimage for months on end. So, how then can you go on a pilgrimage with say, only a week to do it in? Is it even possible?

The answer is, of course! Pilgrimage is more than simply walking from a start point to a finish point, a pilgrimage is a sacred journey taken to ultimately change something inside yourself; to seek physical or psychological healing; it's about escaping the everyday, so you may return from it rested, and feeling different. A pilgrimage, however long it takes, is a journey with intention.

Chapter 3

Pilgrimage within World Religions and Spiritual Paths

Most of the world's main religions have a form of pilgrimage within their devotional practices., Often, visiting a sacred place is linked with a particular time in that religion's calendar, like, the Hajj, for example, which takes place in the last month of the Muslim year. Sometimes a pilgrimage is at a particular time in in an individual's life significant to the religion, or it may be simply that a pilgrimage is expected during the follower's lifetime.

A Hindu pilgrimage often marks a specific phase in the individual's life cycle. The most famous is the festival of Kumbh Mela which takes place by the River Ganges. Every three years, millions of people attend and ritually bathe in the river, led by Holy men, as a means of prāyaścitta (atonement) for past sins. The whole Kumbh Mela festivities last for 55 days and often participants will entertain each other with stories. A common practice is to wear a flower garland which is left in the Ganges as an offering. The origin of the pilgrimage is based on the story of The Garuda – a bird who found a jar of nectar which gave immortality. The Garuda dropped some into the Ganges. Hindu's have numerous gods, and therefore many pilgrimage sites, including Varanasi on the banks of the Ganges. Varanasi is one the oldest inhabited places in the world with over 2,500 years of habitation. It is believed that the god Shiva lived here.

During the three annual pilgrimage festivals of Passover, Shavuot and Sukkoth, Jews might visit the temple of Jerusalem. According to the Jewish tradition, all of creation began in Jerusalem. Although in modern times, pilgrimage is not obligatory in Judaism, millions still visit every year. The Western

Wall is the only remaining part of the second temple, completed in 515 BCE and destroyed in 70 CE by the Romans. The Western Wall is believed to be closest to the presence of God and a symbol of hope that the Jewish people will last forever. Rituals take place here including writing prayers on slips of paper which are pushed into the wall and collected twice a day to be buried at the Mount of Olives. Yad Vasham is a museum and a memorial to the victims of the Holocaust and is situated in Jerusalem. Jewish people who lost members of their families to the Holocaust, visit Yad Vasham as a sign of respect and remembrance.

As previously mentioned in the previous chapter, in Christianity, many people pilgrimage to Jerusalem, the holy lands and any of the sacred places associated with Christ, the apostles or one of the saints. Roman Catholics may pilgrimage to Rome, which is considered by many the centre of their faith, to see the Pope, and hear Mass led by him, especially at Easter. Catholics believe pilgrimage enables them to become closer to God by building a relationship with Him. Protestants, on the other hand, do not believe pilgrimages are necessary, and have in the past, actively opposed pilgrimage believing the veneration of shrines is idolatry.

The Hajj is a mandatory religious duty to all Muslims who are able to complete it, at least once during their lifetime. It takes places annually at the end of the Muslim year. The Hajj is a pilgrimage made to the Kaaba – the House of God – in the city of Mecca, the holiest of places in the Islamic faith. The Hajj includes a series of rituals that must be performed; each person must walk counterclockwise around the Kaaba seven times, walk between the hills of Safa and Marwaha seven times, then drink from the Zamzam well. After this, the pilgrims go to the plains of mount Arafat, to stand vigil, then spend the night in the plain of Muzdalifa, and finally preform the symbolic stoning of the devil by throwing stones at specific pillars.

Pilgrimage is not compulsory in the Sikh religion, and many choose instead to use the money as part of Vand Chhakna, (giving to others in need, and act of generosity.) Other Sikh's believe pilgrimage strengthens their faith, and visit places of significance to the Sikh religion, such as Amritsar, in Punjab, which is the centre of Sikhism and where the Golden Temple, the Harmander Sahib is found. Inside the temple the original holy writings called the Adi Granth are kept. Around 50,000 people from all over the world visit them every day.

Within Buddhism, Pilgrimage may be considered a discipline that fosters spiritual development, or to facilitate a vow taken on recovery from an illness. The prime pilgrimage sites in Buddhism are predominantly in India and Nepal, including the place of Buddha's birth, Lumbini, the place of his enlightenment, Bodh Gaya, Varanasi where he preached his first sermon, and the village of Kushinara recognised as the place of his *parinibbana* (his final death or Nirvana). During the spread of Buddhism, many new sites became centres for pilgrimage and local temples often held festivals.

In other countries, such as China, mountains became famous pilgrim's sites. Often pilgrimage would include stops at sacred places, for example, the Shikoku pilgrimage in Japan, involves visiting eighty-eight temples along its 700-mile route. Most Buddhist pilgrimage sites in Japan are also linked to Shinto shrines. Shinto, the Japanese indigenous religion, is widely considered to be animistic because practitioners believe that Kami inhabit all things from rivers to trees. As with other pilgrimages, there is a distinct overlap in collecting a stamp or seal at each point along the pilgrimage way.

Graham Carter is a practicing Buddhist who runs workshops and retreats for men along with workplace mindfulness sessions. I asked him how he feels about Pilgrimage.

As a Buddhist it isn't something I have specifically considered in relation to my beliefs. As an individual I have always been drawn to going on a pilgrimage. I remember visiting Lourdes about 35 years ago and was fascinated by the journeys the people had been on to get there. Going on a pilgrimage is something I would like to do, and the idea of linking up one or more special / sacred / religious places (be that directly connected to Buddhism, or other faiths, including Paganism) really appeals. Going on a pilgrimage is something I want to initially do on my own – I will use it as a retreat and ensure I have time for reflection, time for meditation, time for being present. I think this will allow me to gain a deeper insight into my own faith as well as my own heart and mind.

When asked where or what sort of pilgrimage he would like to go on, Graham was keen to centre it around Glastonbury, where he enjoys the Shekinah Yoga and Retreat Centre. He is also keen to do part of the route barefoot.

Glastonbury is a centre that is much associated with New Age spirituality and is at the heart of the UK Goddess movement. The movement started during the 1970's as a shift of focus from male dominated religions to the goddess as the prime deity. One of the founders of the goddess movement in Glastonbury is Kathy Jones, who created and lead the annual Goddess conference and instigated the first officially recognised Goddess temple in the UK. The central part of her work is based on the mystical sacred Isle of Avalon and the Goddess in the Glastonbury landscape. Over the years, she has trained and continues to train priests and priestesses in the Avalon traditions.

Visiting Glastonbury, to me, is always an opportunity to refocus my own spirituality, aided by visiting the red spring at the Chalice Well, climbing the impressive Tor and exploring the enigmatic landscape. It is a true balm of sacredness. On one trip, I happened upon one of Kathy Jones' books, *In the nature of*

Avalon – Goddess Pilgrimages in Glastonbury's Sacred landscapes. Written in 1996, it is a comprehensive guide to seeking the goddess and understanding the mythology of Avalon – or Glastonbury. Jones states that these two places, are "only separated by a veil of perspective, how we look at things." She encourages the reader to take pilgrimages to visit places in the area to find the mysterious Avalon and the faces of the Goddess. Within the book are excellent maps, suggestions of routes and details of how to find the different goddess faces.

As I stated, I have been visiting Glastonbury for years, and although I know much of the landscape, I am always intrigued to find an unseen place, and understand new perspectives. I chose to follow part of one of the maps and pilgrimages in the book, *Meandering with the Morgens*. The Nine Morgens, according to Jones, are a sisterhood whose names were recorded by Geoffrey of Monmouth in the twelfth century and were often maligned in Arthurian Myth. They are a mixture of light and dark and triple aspects of various aged women. The pilgrimage takes the walker beyond the Tor and into the less trodden landscapes surrounded by farms and wild areas. The walk in the book begins at Windmill Hill, skirts around chalice hill, and passes along the enigmatically named Hollywell Lane, which Jones says used to lead to an ancient sacred well, (now gone,) then on to the mighty oaks of Gog and Magog, supposed to be 2,000 years old.

The day I set out was early spring and prone to bouts of heavy rain, followed by welcome glimpses of sunshine. To start with, the walk was predominantly along roads which gave me an excellent and enjoyable view of the Tor as I walked past it. The road became a single-track path, and cows were in the fields enjoying the lush grass. The sound of traffic had faded enough to enable deeper contemplation and I focused on my breathing. My footfall echoed on the path, and I could hear the distant sound of a buzzard above. I noted the sodden ground and flooding to the fields as I walked. I began to descend, before me I could see a few houses and a small caravan park to the left. At the bottom of the hill, I turned left through a gate, into a muddy lane, which required care as it was quite boggy. I greeted other walkers heading the other way and finally came upon the enclosure containing Gog and Magog, my primary reason for taking the pilgrimage.

Unfortunately, Gog had already died when Kathy Jones wrote her book, and sadly it appeared that someone had set fire to the tree which was blackened inside. Magog still had new growth along one side, which was heartening to see. I spent a period of time standing with these primeval beings, and although I could not get close due to the fencing, they were a strong presence in the landscape around them. I find when trying to connect with a living being, such as a tree, there is usually a need to physically connect, (by placing a hand on bark etc.) However, their presence was so strong that it did not require this, and I was able to attune to them with ease.

After a time, I followed the Glastonbury Way, a new circular route of 7.5 miles created by the two local councils, up a giant hill towards Paradise Lane. Whilst walking, an owl, disturbed by my footsteps, flew off from a nearby line of bushes as I reached the summit. The view of the Tor was noticeably clear. I then squelched through a field of unassuming cows. Once on the Lane it was an easy route back down towards the town, I stopped at the White Spring to take a small drink of the water, giving thanks for the burst of sunshine.

After years of visiting Glastonbury, time moves differently there. The walk, approx. four miles, felt like it had taken the best part of the day, when in fact it was just over an hour and a half. I decided to try other pilgrimages from Kathy Jones's book, in future visits.

Glastonbury holds a sacredness to other New Age spiritualities, including The Order of Bards, Ovates and Druids, (OBOD) who hold two events there every year, including a ritual on the top of the Tor at the Summer Gathering. Eimear Burke became the chosen chief of OBOD in 2020 at the height of the pandemic. It is one of the oldest and most prominent Druid groups in the UK and across the world. Living in Kilkenny, Ireland, and having spent years working in counselling and psychology, Eimear co-founded the Kilkenny Druid college with her late husband. Eimear plays the harp and is a mentor for Italian members of OBOD.

On OBOD's website, you will find much information on pilgrimage, along with many other aspects of Druidry. It explains that Druids hold and treat all of nature as sacrosanct. Sacred sites have significance, especially if along ley lines or ancient tracks created by our ancestors. I recently spoke to Eimear about pilgrimage and Druidry. I asked her what pilgrimage means to her.

It's tapping into magic, tapping into the spirit of the place, the land or the landscape, and each stop along the way has a different story to tell depending how open you are to it." She says, *"Everyone's journey is so different.* She continued... *Myself and a friend who's also a Druid went on a retreat in Donegal (Ireland) last April, around the Birog a druidess who gets two little mentions in the epic battle of Moytura, yet she ensures that Lugh (the God) is conceived and then saves his life in order to fulfil a prophecy. We held the retreat in the landscape in which the story takes place – we found her rock, we found her cave, we found the various elements of the story. It's around immersing yourself in the story, while immersing yourself in the landscape. This is a pilgrimage, and it starts when you pack your bags.*

A Pilgrimage isn't just a nice holiday, on pilgrimage we're often confronted by a struggle, I remember going to Iona, and having to cross three bodies of water, from Ireland to Scotland, across to Mull and then to Iona. There were delays and it involved a bit of hardship and a bit of challenge, which helps you tap into your own wisdom and your own resources and resilience, which is part of a pilgrimage as well. It's about being able to engage with the challenges you meet along the way. Then You'll come back, hopefully renewed hopefully in a spiritual sense you'll be renewed in some way. You may have let go of many things but taken on a new perspective.

I asked Eimear about her own intentional pilgrimages. She told me she has travelled with her friends who set up Brigid's Way, a pilgrim route in Ireland in 2013. The route begins where Brigid was born and ends at her monastery in Kildare where she passed away.

I Climbed Kilimanjaro, which is not seen as a pilgrimage in the strictest sense, but we were entering into sacred space, it wasn't about conquering the mountain, it was about engaging with the spirits of the mountain so we could succeed. I did ceremonies along the way, I didn't sleep, I would stay awake meditating on peace, and dealing with the altitude. It was very profound. My friend said I should leave my baggage at the bottom of the mountain, don't bring it up with you. As we ascended the last bit, at night, I was aware of going in and out of my body, I took one step and a peace prayer, and I felt I was still up on the mountain for months afterwards.

I went to Lourdes, when I was seventeen, my father used to volunteer there as a doctor, and when myself or my siblings left school, would go with a group of young people on a bus and help in the town. I wasn't the least bit interested in the religious aspect and it didn't call to me at all, but we had fun. So that was an official pilgrimage that was not a pilgrimage for me although it's very important for people of the (Roman catholic) faith.

With Druid Pilgrimage, to a sacred site, built say 5,000 years ago, we haven't got any dogma, although there maybe myths and stories around it. You are free to engage with it or not. There may be different manifestations or associations with the place, it's still very much a personal experience, that's not to say going to Lourdes isn't a personal thing but there's a structure and definite narrative about it, that people follow.

As a Druid do you visit a sacred site in the sense of a pilgrimage or just to connect to the place?

I think that's up to you, if you go as a tourist, you get one thing out of it, but if you go in pilgrimage, you get far more out of it, it lends a greater richness to it. My sense it, from speaking to Druid friends is that you don't go superficially to visit a place, they've gone with a sense of reverence or awe and a sense of curiosity or magic. It's never, I've been there, I took a photograph and I left. Invariably there's some kind of story of their experience, for example, they were drawn to a particular stone, or they felt sick or healed, for example. I think if you go in in a more mindful way, if you leave yourself open, things happen. You go and the place will reveal itself to you.

How did you feel after the pilgrimages that felt more profound to you? How were you effected when you returned to your life?

I think it was a sense of letting go of stuff and being cleansed and renewed. There was a subtle sense of something having shifted and healed.

A lot of people who do modern pilgrimages don't walk in the sense of how you used to do in medieval times. How do you feel about this?

There's always a qualitative difference between walking, being on a bike, on a horse or in a car going through a landscape. I have a camper van that I love driving to places and seeing things from a different perspective, but it's still at speed. We don't have time these days to devote three years to doing a pilgrimage, however there is something to be said for walking that can't be compensated for. However, if it was only walking then people who are unable to wouldn't be able to go. I think it's not just about the physical journey but the internal one too. When I'm walking (in pilgrimage) I like to walk for some of the way in silence to appreciate your own inner journey. So, if you can't walk, that inner journey is all the more important. I don't think there's any hard and fast rules.

We discussed the idea of pilgrimage as a life journey, and Eimear told me she has a labyrinth in her garden.

Around the 1600s it was very popular in churches. That was a symbolic journey to the Holy Land because not everybody could afford to go on a pilgrimage, timewise or financially. People would walk the labyrinth and meet Jesus in the middle. It could be done every day or every week, it was the symbolic in and out of pilgrimage space. A pilgrimage is not linear, there's not always a straight line and you can stop and start again. I think the important one (pilgrimage) is the interior one.

I thanked Eimear for her insight into Druidry and pilgrimage. If anyone is interested in learning more about Eimear's work and her retreat/pilgrimage with Birog in Donegal please visit her website at *www.kilkennydruidry.com*. Alternatively, if you are interested in OBOD and Druidry in general please visit: *https. druidry.org*

Scott Richardson-Reed, a folk magic practitioner, living in the wonderful Scottish borders, is the creator of the blog and website, the Cailleach's Herbarium, which primarily offers information and resources on Scottish folklore folk magic and herbalism. I have had the good fortune to meet Scott several times and participate in the Taibhsear Collective run events on folklore and magic in Edinburgh and online during the pandemic. (*www.taibhsearcollective.com*) I was keen to find out what Scott thinks about the concept of pilgrimage from both his spiritual viewpoint and his own personal one. As we spoke, he told me about his interest in Tigh Nan Bodach an ancient pagan shrine in the valley of Glen Lyon in Perthshire, reputed to honour the ancient Goddess, the Cailleach

Pilgrimage does in a way hold a special place in my practice. It was taking a pilgrimage up to see the Tigh Nan Bodach, which became the inspiration for my writing and focus on reciprocity and land use. The Pilgrimage to the Tigh na Bodach was a very special moment for me, and I've since been back twice with other people. It was at the very early start of me exploring Scottish folk magic and traditional practices. I had no idea why I needed to go there; I figured it might be nice to be able to provide a wee account of the place for others who may wish to do the same.

I've always been drawn to the Cailleach in our landscape and so set off hopeful that we would have good weather. You can read about the journey on my website but once there it was a very peaceful moment, the sun breaking over the nearby Munro... A moment of repose I guess you might call it. In terms of its impact on my practice it's a little nebulous, we have hopes when we travel to places like this we will be touched by the miraculous or something significant will happen. I did feel at peace, and I did feel like I had honoured a promise and maybe that was received in a reciprocal way too. There was a feeling of walking the walk and keeping our word I think echoes through a lot of folk magic and animist based practices.

I asked Scott what the impact of the pilgrimage had on his own personal and spiritual practice.

One impact of the journey was I felt more inspired than ever to write and the Imbas or inspiration was really easy to access, ideas flowed a lot faster, and it was a time I could write for long periods

26

and lots of new ideas would come effortlessly. I think in answer to your question in a way is yes, feeling inspired whether because of the locale, or the journey, or something more internal, definitely happened but what was responsible for that I'm not sure – something in me or something other. It happened I guess that's all that matters.

I think each long walk-in nature I take with a destination in mind becomes a sort of pilgrimage. After I became really unwell with sepsis, I took a really long walk into our local area to ruminate and think on things heading to a local hawthorn tree and back again.

I enquired if he had any plans to visit further sacred sites when he is able to.

Hopefully this year I'm going to follow the path of St Cuthbert on a pilgrimage of sorts, though following the path of the saint isn't for the saint, (in a Christian sense) but more so to connect with a saint associated with place. I can't think of a better way to connect to the land you are on than following an old track like that.

I think I'm looking for a similar experience with the St Cuthbert route – seeking inspiration and the calm that comes with it. There is the reason for contemplative reflection whilst I'm walking the path he once took and also visiting and potentially marking places that have a quality about them, I can return to or that need some TLC like sacred wells et which might have at one time been a bigger feature of the route. There is also walking the land I live on, and I think pilgrimage routes are a really effective way of doing this. The saints of old a lot of the time hide a deeper aspect that came before them and it's maybe exploring this aspect with my own embodiment and how my body, psyche and spirit respond to the land that's an important aspect of it for me personally.

I guess I'm saying it's not so much the destination but the journey that's important, though I'm sure the destination is beautiful, and I'll enjoy it a lot, especially its deep history and resonance within the place I currently call home.

For more information about all Scott's work please visit his website, The Cailleach's Herbarium, *(www.cailleachs-herbarium. com)* and on Facebook – and keep an eye on his website for further events from the Taibhsear Collective on Facebook.

Moving on from here, I approached a friend and fellow Heilung lover, Andre Henriques. Andre is a Heathen, and tutor at Treadwell's Bookshop, in London, for whom he regularly runs workshops on the Runes, Seidr and Heathen Gods, He holds Heathen rituals within the community, both locally and internationally. I asked Andre what pilgrimage means to him and how it manifests in Heathenry.

The idea of pilgrimage means to be a journey to a sacred or special site, be it natural or with historical significance. Going to a forest int the UK can be a pilgrimage. Going to the Netherlands to a pagan festival is a pilgrimage to me. It's the journey there and back, and how it changes you and enriches you, that is a pilgrimage to me. Any pilgrimage in Northern Europe is to me a Heathen pilgrimage. Other Heathens will have different views on this.

I asked Andre to tell me about his own experiences of pilgrimage.

My first pilgrimage was when living in Portugal, I went camping alone in the mountains in the North. It was some kind of Vision Quest at the time. I was chased by big dogs that looked like wolves, it was miles from anywhere with big storms and thundering mountains all around me. It was the first time I felt truly alive. At the time, it was a rite of passage, I had finished my degree and was starting my professional life soon. It was so good I did many others after, especially to Northern Europe.

How would you sum up pilgrimage to you as a Heathen?

Pilgrimage was, and still is, a way of finding myself, allowing space for insight and inspiration to come, and to connect with Nature, ancestors, and Gods. It is definitely part of my spiritual processes of transformation.

One thing that is common throughout most religions and paths of spirituality, is that pilgrimage is accepted as a means to achieve a unique transcendent awareness that cannot be achieved any other way. I would go as far as to say that pilgrimage in one of its forms, is a natural progression, and even a widespread need by those spiritually enlightened. I am Hopeful that from reading this chapter you find inspiration from those I spoke to, and your interest will have been piqued enough to examine these very different paths, yet with similar aspects in their approach to pilgrimage.

Chapter 4

Tools to Help You

Some people, (myself included) keep a journal or two for varying reasons. I have one, a general journal that I write in fairly frequently, this is filled with things I have been doing, inspirational thoughts, and it is often a place where I work through something that has concerned me or caused me anxiety. I have found this is a great way to see things from a different perspective, and to vent any feelings in a safe personal way. I also tend to doodle and draw in this journal, sometimes adding a picture or two, maybe a photograph or something that has inspired me, and I may want to re-visit at a later time. This is a very personal type of journal and one I don't share with others.

I also have a creative writing journal, which I use when I attend an event or creative writing workshops, for example. This is full of ideas and thoughts, as well as snippets of poems and words from other writers which have particularly resonated with me. Sometimes I may see an object and really want to record it and my thoughts around it, so I may draw and write or add a picture here and there. This is quite a scruffy journal because it is stuffed with bits, loose sheets and sometimes materials. I tend to be a visual journal keeper.

In Andrew Anderson's highly recommended book, *The Ritual of Writing*, He states that he has at least three journals and diaries for various reasons, but primarily to hone his writing technique and reflect upon his progress both in writing and spiritually. The reason I am talking about journaling and diary keeping is because I am hoping you may be considering creating a journal or book about your pilgrimage and your journey to it. I have found it an immensely helpful tool to find my own authentic voice and to plot my journey, both in a more spiritual way within myself and a physical one. It's a great place to jot down ideas, make notes and even glue in timetables!

However, it may seem daunting, especially if you have never been one to write regularly before, or it may have been a long time since you did. The best strategy is to start simply; either buy or re-purpose a notebook or use an online word processor and try writing at least a sentence a day for a week or two. Hopefully during this time, you will notice that you want to write more and may even want to include your thoughts or write about something that happened to you. You may feel inspired by seeing a documentary about your longed-for place, for example, and want to compose your thoughts so as to reflect later or come up with plans of action. All these things are tools that can be used to aid your pilgrimage and journal writing skills. Perhaps you are an aspiring artist, and wish to illustrate your words, or an image you find in a magazine grabs your attention? Cut it out and stick it in your notebook or make a representation of it in pencil or paint. Anderson suggests that you take your diary to a wild place or somewhere in nature, (I would add maybe a place of special significance to you). Try writing about what you see, feel, and hear. Does it feel different writing outside as opposed to indoors?

After a couple of weeks, take a look at what you have created and reflect upon how journaling may be of help to you on your pilgrimage journey.

When I was creating my own pilgrimage journal, I was strongly inspired to craft something special with words, however, although I enjoy reading poetry, I felt far from confident in constructing my own poems, so decided to try my hand at Haiku.

As you may know, Haiku originated in Japan and is a short seventeen syllable form of prose/poem. In English this is usually broken down into three lines of 5,7,5 syllables, whereas in the original Japanese works, they were often on a single line, and originally part of a larger poem called a Renga. The modern form of Haiku became popular in Japan during the seventeenth century thanks to Japanese master Matsuo Basho and often reflected single moments in the natural world, for example:

古池や蛙飛びこむ水の音

furu ike ya / kawazu tobikomu / mizu no oto

which translates as:

an ancient pond / a frog jumps in / the splash of water.

Haiku became known in the Western world during the nineteenth century, with some translations into English and French, but its popularity really took off in the early twentieth century largely thanks to R.H Blyth, a renowned academic in Japanese Literature, who translated many Haiku into English and wrote extensively about them. This in turn kindled the popularity of the writing of Haiku in English.

So Why Haiku? In essence Haiku is the very heart of a poem, the centre point of meaning in all its vivacity. Haiku are often enigmatic, a moment of time which leaves the reader to contemplate and consider the layers of meaning of each carefully chosen word. The creation of Haiku is a very precise craft and requires complete attention to both the subject and the form. Further to this, it allows the slowing of the pace of life and the appreciation of a moment. It is an excellent way of honing word skills and enhancing your writing ability.

Once you have crafted your own Haiku it can be used as a mediative focus, and a memory of the moment it was written. Your Haiku are exactly that: yours, so you can keep them

entirely to yourself, for your own personal use. I don't claim
be to be any good at writing them, but I do find it a useful tool
to aid my focus and explore my own imagination. Here is one I
wrote whilst reflecting on my visit to Iona:

My Iona is...
Silver sand and azure sea
Holy green stone tears

My Iona is...
Marbled well of wet faced Bride
Dream Columba's Peace

Perhaps you might like to write poems about your place instead?
Some pilgrims create artworks, or mood boards to explore their
journey, and use this as an inspirational springboard into their
pilgrimages. Whatever tools you find helps you focus and create
your own unique pilgrimage that is special to you.

Literary pilgrimages that weren't

Okay this title needs explaining. Often when reading in general
I have come across journeys – sometimes fictional but often real
life or based upon true events – that although not considered
a pilgrimage in the strictest sense, still have key features of
pilgrimage and could have been called so. I hope that makes
sense.

In 1878 a young man sets off with a donkey to hike alone
through the sparsely populated Cevennes Mountain range in
Southwest France. His reason is to distance himself from a love
affair that has fallen through, and effectively broken his heart.
His twelve-day journey covers over 200 km. As he travels, he is
often mistaken for a peddler and when the locals discover he
isn't, they are horrified that he should want to sleep outside,

away from towns and civilisation. Robert Louis Stevenson remains mentally detached from their protestations, stating:

> For my part, I travel not to go anywhere, but to go. I travel for travel's sake. The great affair is to move; to feel the needs and hitches of our life more clearly; to come down off this feather-bed of civilization, and find the globe granite underfoot and strewn with cutting flints....To hold a pack upon a pack-saddle against a gale out of the freezing north is no high industry, but it is one that serves to occupy and compose the mind. And when the present is so exacting who can annoy himself about the future?

Indeed, Stevenson makes every effort not to think about his love, (Fanny Osborne, an older divorced American woman whom his friends and family disapproved of, whom he later marries,) and certainly not write about it.

> Even in the journal, (from which he later writes the book) he suppressed most of his real feelings, and disguises the fact that, alone in the mountains, he was savouring Fanny's departure undisturbed. (Calder. Jenni. RLS A Life Study. 1980. p.120.)

The journey, wild camping, as it would be called today, over a fair distance, "...was of course excellent therapy, to have taken on a professional exercise at a time of emotional disruption." (Calder. Jenni. RLS a Life Study. 1980.p.120.) and enabled Stevenson to return to his life in Edinburgh to write the book, along with other great works.

Similarly, in 2013, Raynor Winn and her husband Moth, who has been diagnosed with a terminal condition, decided to walk the Southwest Coast path. In *The Salt Path*, they have been made homeless after losing a legal battle, and literally have nowhere to go, so decide to walk. After a hesitant start, with little money and wild camping along the way, Moth slowly began to move with more ease: *"I'm stronger, I feel as though I can put one foot in front of the other and trust where it'll land..."* (165) believing the "extreme physio" has made all the difference to his condition. As they walk, they begin to really appreciate the landscape around them, and live in the moments. One particular scene has both swimming in the sea in the moonlight, when Moth encourages Ray to swim underwater with her eyes open. *"Instead of murky darkness, there were showers of white and silver...moving swaying refracting through the water..."* (192) At the end of their journey, Ray realises what a gift she has been given: *"...I understood what homelessness has done for me. It had taken every material thing that I had and left me stripped bare...It had also given me a choice...I chose hope."* (272)

Walking the South-West coast path helps author Katherine May come to terms with her recent Autism diagnosis in *The Electricity of Every Living Thing*. While exploring the wild landscapes on weekends, she begins to understand why she had found everyday life so difficult to cope with, and the nature of difference. Although not walking all of the path in one continuous go, May begins to find that the hectic nature of family, work and social life are left behind, it gives her focus: *"When I walk, a space opens up, and I can finally perceive the fine texture of my own life. It's like dropping through a trapdoor into another world; my world."* (p.204).

Moving now to the coast of Ireland and Scotland, Philip Marsden's dramatic journey to the Summer Isles along the west coast in an old yacht is a beautiful story of the places along the way, his own quest to understand the loss of his Aunt Bridget and to fulfil their dream of reaching the Summer Isles together. As the story of his journey unfolds, his love of the myths and legends of place enable him to understand his aunt's death and begin to come to terms with it. *"This book is about such places –*

*places drawn by longing and memory, places just beyond our reach...
and it's about what happens when you set sail in search of them.*" (13)

So here I have shown examples of journeys that aren't
pilgrimages but, in some sense, could have been called so. I
seem to gravitate towards books with journeys or life changing
experiences in, and these are just a sample to whet your appetite.

A few other books that feature journeys which you might
find interesting:

To The Island of Tides (A Journey to Lindisfarne) Alistair Moffat.
The Frayed Atlantic Edge David Gange.
Love of Country. (A Hebridean Journey) Madeline Bunting.
The Old Ways – A journey on Foot Robert Macfarlane.
Dart Alice Oswald.
The Ravens Nest Sarah Thomas.
Arabia – a Journey Through the Hearth of the Middle East
Levison Wood.
And there are lots more.

- Browse the travel section of your local bookshop, or
  library and pick up a book that interests you.
- Read travel blogs and magazines, try to look beyond your
  comfort zone, and challenge yourself to discover new
  experiences.
- What do you find inspiring?
- Do the books/articles fill you with a sense of longing or
  dread?
- Write about it in your journal.

Chapter 5

Labyrinths and Mazes

I am guessing most have at least a basic knowledge of the story of the Minotaur in Greek Mythology. As I child I was given a book of Greek myths and I absolutely loved the stories. I clearly remember that on the cover was the image of the Minotaur – a beast that was supposed to be half man and half bull. In case you aren't familiar with the story, here is a brief summary:

The story goes that the Minotaur was imprisoned in a complex labyrinth, designed by Daedalus, underneath the King Minos's palace at Knossos. Every year a tribute of seven young men and seven young women was sent from Athens in way of compensation for killing Minos' son Androgeus. These youths were cast into the labyrinth and eaten by the Minotaur.

One year Theseus, a prince of Athens, arrived with the tribute, with the intention of killing the minotaur and freeing the other youths. Ariadne, daughter of King Minos, fell in love with Theseus and smuggled him a sword, along with a ball of red thread to enable him to find his way out of the labyrinth. Of course, you have probably guessed, the hero killed the Minotaur, freed the other Athenians, and took Ariadne away with him.

The myth is based around the idea of the labyrinth as a prison for the Minotaur, and that this is situated below the palace at Minos. In the 1800s Knossos was discovered on Crete, a Greek island in the Mediterranean. In 1900 an English Archaeologist, Arthur Evans, began excavating the site, which lasted for thirty-five years. The site was far bigger than anyone had anticipated and included the discovery of two ancient writing scripts, along with numerous treasures, including some beautiful fresco fragments. Evans came up with the theory that what he was excavating was the Minoan palace of King Minos himself. This hypothesis has always been seen as contentious, especially as there is little evidence of the all-important labyrinth.

I expect you are wondering what this has to do with pilgrimage at all. Let me explain, firstly with a little history. During the Medieval period when pilgrimage was at the height of its popularity, not all people could go on a long-distance pilgrimage for many reasons, such as health, finances and being unable to leave their homes or loved ones. Churches and cathedrals began to etch large floor labyrinths or build turf labyrinth in their grounds. These were known as "The path to Jerusalem" or a symbol of pilgrimage. Many drawings and etchings from the eighteenth and nineteenth century, show parishioners in deep meditative states traversing these labyrinths, apparently in communion with the divine. Today, one of the most famous is Chartres Cathedral in France, situated in the nave and over 12m in size with over 260m of paths to follow. In my local area there is what is known as a "Miz Maze" on top of one of the tallest hills. A Miz Maze is actually a labyrinth rather than a maze, and similar in style to traditional Troy-town style turf labyrinth. It is possible that this turf designed labyrinths or Miz Maze were more commonplace during the medieval period, and one is even mentioned in Shakespeare's *A Midsummers Night Dream* by the faerie queen Titania, *"And the quaint mazes in the wanton green..."*

I have spent hours quietly walking the Miz Maze on St Catherine's Hill near Winchester, following the paths in deep contemplation, reaching the centre, before turning out again. It is an excellent mindfulness tool and a great way to do a walking meditation.

Interestingly, these types of labyrinths are called a Troy-town labyrinth, alluding to the mythical city of Troy. There is some academic thought that these are the original and is possibly one of the most ancient forms of labyrinth. A fine

example of this can be found at Rocky Valley, near Tintagel in Cornwall, carved into the rocks as you head to the sea. These carvings are probably dated between the early Bronze-Age (3300–2100 BCE) and Iron Age (500 BCE to 200 CE) although other theorists suggest they may be later. Nevertheless, they are enigmatic and add to the mystery of the area. The ageless design of the labyrinth brings me back to the story of the Minotaur, the Cretan Palace of Knossos, and the mystery of its famous mythological labyrinth. Recently the Ashmolean Museum in Oxford, UK had an exhibition about Knossos and the Labyrinth, which I was fortunate to attend.

The exhibition looked at the myth surrounding Knossos as Minos and the excavations conducted by Arthur Evans, who speculated that they were one and the same. With over

two hundred artifacts, (one hundred of them on loan from Greece,) I was looking forward to seeing rare items and hoping to finally answer the question of the location of the mythic labyrinth. The myth of the labyrinth has led to thousands of visitors to Knossos every year. In the first room of the exhibition, visitors were greeted by a beautiful section of a fresco from

Knossos and various labyrinthine designs including rare coins with the design, alongside a Roman statue of a bull-headed monster. Following the rooms, brought you to sumptuous replicas of decadent rooms and even the supposed throne of Minos. However, as I walked along with everyone else in eager anticipation, delving deeper into the archaeological evidence, the mysterious labyrinth which once housed the minotaur became more remote. There were beautiful artifacts including copies of the infamous snake goddess, and the much-admired octopus' vases. Further along, I viewed a plan and model of the layout of the palace, and everything became that much more enigmatic again. Could the palace itself have been the labyrinth or the inspiration for the myth? It was one of those unanswered questions thatleft the visitor with more questions than answers.

Let's go back to the uses of labyrinths as a tool for pilgrimage, one way is as a focus in meditation:

Sit yourself (or lie) somewhere comfortable where you will not be disturbed and if it helps you to go into a deeper state, light a candle. Take deep breaths and follow your own method of deepening your state of meditation. When you are ready, picture the labyrinth in your mind, take a few moments or breaths to fully see the whole labyrinth form. Then, allow yourself to slowly begin walking or following its paths. This may take a couple of minutes but take your time and feel yourself becoming immersed in the flow of the lines. Imagine that this is your path in a spiritual pilgrimage and allow your mind to take you along. When you come to the centre, pause, take deep breaths, and focus on arriving at your pilgrimage destination. This is your centre, the place you have always been heading towards. Feel your emotions and the completeness of this stage of your spiritual pilgrimage.

When you are ready, begin to follow the lines of the labyrinth and your path back towards the outside world. Contemplate what you will bring back with you into your life. As you reach

the end, begin to hear the world around you, feel your body, and
surroundings beneath and around you. Gently open your eyes and
refocus on your candle. Take a sip of water to ground yourself and
write your experience in your journal.

I have a beautiful clay hand labyrinth in the Troy-town style, which sits proudly next to my desk and sometimes near to my bed. I use it in mindfulness and meditation work and would recommend it. To use in mediation, as above close your eyes, take deep breaths, and allow your fingers to follow the lines to the centre and return out again. I find this every calming and relaxing, especially after a busy day.

I particularly like drawing and creating labyrinths and find it a highly effective mindful exercise. It could be something you add to your journal or use to enable a deeper meditation practice. Please see below on a simple way of doing so. I have also made them outside with organic materials, such as autumn leaves and stones on a beach. This has the added bonus of being impermanent, so has little impact on the natural world, but a great impact on mental health and focus.

Whichever way you choose to use labyriths, if at all, I believe it with be conducive to a deeper and more personally satifying pigrimage when you come to do it.

Chapter 6

Longing and Calling

Longing

.... folk long to go on pilgrimages
To tread new shores . . . to seek shrines far away.
(Chaucer. The Canterbury Tales.)

Maybe you have felt a longing or yearning for a while now? To step away from your busy all consuming, time pressured life, to just be? Perhaps you yearn for space and freedom from the distractions of technology.

Paulo Coelho states in his book *The Pilgrimage*:

Maybe the journey isn't so much about becoming anything. Maybe it's about unbecoming everything that isn't really you.

In this case, longing is distinctly different from desire, which is to want or covet something you already know of and is achievable. For example, you might desire or want to go on holiday, where you'll get a good tan, eat great food, and spend time with your family. Longing, in this instance, I would describe as something less corporeal, more wishful, and mysterious.

Something inside you just wants to go on a pilgrimage but we don't really know why. We feel a need to find something within ourselves but aren't sure what exactly. You have grown weary of the way our lives are now and want to have new experiences to enable us to find a change in outlook or gain a new perspective. You are in a conundrum and are looking for clarity.

In short, a pilgrimage maybe the key to transformation, or inner growth you are looking for. If you picked this book up, then you must be already thinking pilgrimage, and it could be the answer to your longing.

When I was considering my pilgrimage to Iona, I tried various techniques to give my initial ambiguity a sense of certainty. The first thing I did was to practice mindfulness. Mindfulness means being fully aware of every moment and paying attention to the present. It does sounds far easier than it is. Our lives are so full of distractions, that we often don't notice what's going on around us. We tend to get so caught up in our own thoughts, or with what's happening on Facebook, that we lose awareness of everything else. Taking a few simple steps can overcome this and allow us to live in the moment and understand our thoughts and emotions better.

A simple daily routine of one or two of these, can be effective to our inner clarity.

1. When you wake up in the morning, rather than jumping straight out of bed, concentrate on your senses.
   What can you hear?
   It might be your alarm clock, or a radio, perhaps you can hear traffic, or a child....
   What can you feel?
   The bed clothes against your skin, the warmth of the bed.
   What can you see?
   Is it the digits on your clock, or the sunshine peeping through the curtains?
   What can you smell?
   Coffee brewing downstairs.
   What can you taste?
   Your mouth might be dry and salty.
   Pause on each of these sensations before you start your day.

2. Take three breaths.
   In the morning before breakfast, go outside, even in the rain. Stand somewhere pleasant and take three slow breaths.
   The first looking at the sky above you.
   The second looking at the earth and ground beneath you.
   The third looking around you.

3. Try something new
   Sit in a different place in a meeting or have something you've never eaten before for lunch. Eat outside or read a book instead of staying in and watching TV.

4. Go bare foot.
   Walk outside without a covering on your feet. Notice the textures of the path, grass, stones. Fell the earth underneath you, the damp grass, and the cool stone. Enjoy the sensations.

5. Before you go to sleep, close your eyes but be aware of your other senses. Can you hear or smell anything? Are the covers warm and relaxing? Concentrate on these sensations before you fall asleep. If thoughts come up to distract you, remind yourself that these are just thoughts.

Try to do one or two of these simple techniques every day, this will help you become more present in the moment. If you have trouble stopping thoughts and things popping into your head, try thinking of them as though they are buses and you are simply watching them come and go without getting on them. This might seem tricky at first but persevere. Another technique is to name your thoughts, for example: change "I might not be able to get my point across when talking to my mum and will fail" thought to "this is anxiety." In this way you are distancing yourself and objectifying the feeling, thus making it easier not to become distracted, overwhelmed or engulfed by it.

If you find mindfulness helpful, then you might consider developing a more formal mindful practice. Mindful meditation involves concentrating on your breathing and its sensations, throughout your body whilst bringing your attention back if mind begins to wander. I would also recommend Qi Gong and Tai Chi as meditative practices that raise awareness of both your bodies' movement and you're breathing. Please note though that these practices will probably not be instantaneous, they are definitely worth persevering with.

By far the most helpful practice I have found to aid me in bringing lucidity and finding answers to the more elusive questions is walking! Getting out into the fresh air, being in the landscape – a park, somewhere with trees and greenery. Absorb the signs of the changing seasons, smell the air around you after it has rained, notice how the leaves change colour in subtle ways depending on the light – all these things bring that all important connection to the world and nature. Walking allows you to step away from the artificialness of society, it gets you fit and healthy and allows you to clear your head of all the distractions that fill up your precious time. I am going to make the leap of assumption and say if you are considering doing a pilgrimage, even if it's just a thought at the moment, then you probably like walking/being out in the landscape or already have a walking routine, or regular visits to a natural habitat in your life.

Walking in meditation or mindfully, has certain advantages if you struggle with concentrating in still (like seated or lying down positions,) meditation. The difficultly is that the mind is more likely to wander when there is little stimulation. When walking, the mind has more sensory input, and it's therefore easier to focus. The rhythmic movement of the body is a great meditation inducer, in much the same way as drumming does, and also brings the rhythm of your body back into sync. The sensations, sounds, smells, and sights while we walk, help to bring grounding to our minds, bringing every part of our body into balance and order.

Here are some simple Mindful walking exercises to help you get started:

1. Your Feet.

   Firstly, find somewhere where you can stand uninterrupted or disturbed for a few minutes.

   Close your eyes.

   Focus on the part of your body with the most powerful sensations, (Probably your feet). How do they feel? Tired? Warm? How does the ground (or shoe) feel beneath them?

   Slowly lift one foot.

   Observe the way it feels.

   Notice as you roll onto the front of your foot and lift it off the ground completely.

   Your Foot is free. How does it feel?

   Bring your foot slowly back down onto the ground. What sensations do you feel?

   Repeat with the other foot.

2. One word.

   Start by standing with your eyes closed. Think about the sensations you are feeling in your body. Label each feeling you notice, but only use one word. For example, if you are wearing a hat, it could be "warm" or even "cooling."

   Begin to walk, slowly and label each feeling, and when you feel more confident, begin to add one word for each physical action you take in walking, e.g., "bending" your knee.

Gradually your mind will sharpen, and this newfound awareness will fill your body with previously unnoticed feelings and sensations.

Mindful walking becomes a flow through your body.

3. Senses

   Use your five senses to become aware of your surroundings and how they react with you. Focus on each sense, one at a time.

   Fell the warmth of the sun on your face.

   Hear the soft movement of wind in the tree leaves.

   Smell the saltiness of the sea.

   Taste the air.

   See the beautiful vivid red flowers dancing in the breeze.

There are three stages to walking meditation:

Concentration

Attention

Insight.

This third step is gained through achieving the first two and may lead us to clarity and bring understanding to our longing.

Calling

In the introduction I spoke about my dream of a place that I had when young, although it was many years before it manifested into reality. The persistence of the memory and strength of the imagery stayed in my subconscious even when I had pushed it aside, and had almost forgotten about it, assuming it to be… well, a dream. Much later in my life, by chance, I finally found the place I had been called to, (Iona) through a TV programme of all things.

If I could explain this further, I would use the analogy of looking at a scene through the viewfinder of an analogue camera, out of focus and blurred until you adjust the lens and suddenly everything becomes sharp and clear to you.

I am hoping that by recounting my experience, this may stir something within you. Have you had a dream in a similar way to me and are searching to find it, or maybe you have come across an image or seen a place on a TV programme that really resonates with you? It maybe something more abstract than that. Does the name of a location stir a recollection within you, or you are drawn to somewhere on a map?

If this is the case, then I am going to suggest that you do research on the place that pulls you to it. By all means look the place up online and spend time perusing images or even watch clips and films on YouTube. I would recommend a library search, (if you have one nearby) or visit your local bookshop and see what books you can find in relation to a pilgrimage to this area. Have you got friends who have been to this place? Ask them about their experiences and get them to show you their pictures!

Consider starting a journal, as a journey towards the place and your feelings in relation to it. Collect images – photos or artworks and quotes that inspire you in your call. Find articles in magazines online or physically and add them with your own thoughts and ideas. The place may invite you to become creative – from writing poetry to painting pictures. Express your inner most thoughts and desires regarding your calling to the place. Gradually as you begin to fill the journal, you will see the journey you are making internally towards your calling place.

If the location is already a pilgrimage site, then there will definitely be online blogs or websites dedicated to it, and you may find that other pilgrims experiences or observations further stimulate your own. I remember reading a blog from a fellow pilgrim to Iona before I left, although they went with primarily a Christian ethos, which was not in line with my own thinking, nevertheless I was not only reassured that my belief in my own intuition was validated, but I was able to find inspiration from their words. In a sense their pilgrimage also became my inner pilgrimage, giving me ideas of things to experience, and sometimes different perspective to consider.

But what if you have not experienced a pull or call to anywhere specific yet? You might be worried that you will not gain the fulfilment that you are looking for, whether this is spiritual insight or answers to those questions from simply randomly going to a place.

The following mediation may help you to clarify your calling if it remains elusive to you:

Find somewhere comfortable to be seated, (or lay) which will not be disturbed. You could put on soothing meditative music or light a candle, or incense to help you relax. Make sure your clothing is comfortable and will not irritate you while you meditate, and you are not too hot or cold.

Sit in a position that you will be able to maintain for a short period of time, if you are unused to meditating, then I would recommend some sort of back support, and that rather than sitting directly on the floor, you sit on a cushion or even in your favourite chair or lay down but be aware you might fall asleep.

Close your eyes and take a slow deep breath in through your nose, make it fill your stomach, and slowly let it out through your mouth. Repeat and as you breath out feel all the tensions and worries flow out with your breaths. Concentrate on the feelings within your body, of fullness on the intake and emptiness on the out breath. Allow your mind to settle into stillness. Repeat breathing this way until you feel sufficiently still and content.

Now imagine a beautiful golden light surrounding your body, and feel the tingle as it touches and works through you, starting at your feet, gradually up your legs to your body, feel the protecting and shimmering golden light climb your spine to your neck and shoulders down your arms into your hands and fingers, each shining with golden light. The light fills your mind and face as it reaches the top of your head and your whole body feels alive with shining shimmering golden light. The light flows from you now and feel your mind flowing along with it, through the air and above the clouds across the vast skies. Enjoy the sensation of flying like a spec of golden light. You look down on seas and mountains and see birds flying along on the airstreams with you, you feel at peace and at one with the world.

As you fly through the air, you feel a slight pull in a slightly different direction, follow this sensation to where it leads you... over towns and forests or vast oceans and deserts to somewhere that draws you to it. Gently let yourself be guided by this feeling as you come closer to the area that calls you...it may seem slightly disorientating or fuzzy as you come gradually down to the ground.

Looks around you, absorb what you see and feel. Drink in the smells and taste the air. How does it feel under your feet as you begin moving, is it grassy or a path? Follow your instinct as you explore the area. Are there other people or animals around you? Try speaking to one of them, ask them what this place is. Listen carefully to what they say.

Continue exploring and enjoying the place you have been called to for as long as you feel you want to.

After a while, when you feel ready, you begin to slowly return to the starting point at which you landed. You feel yourself gently lifting up into the air, as things start to blur around you. You rise back into the sky filled with golden light and return towards the way you arrived, enjoying the warmth of the golden sun and the views over the seas and mountains below. Slowly sense the golden shimmering light returning into your body. Gently begin to feel the sensations in your face and neck and gradually down your spine into your legs. Become aware of your breathing –steadily in through your nose and out through your mouth. You become aware of the music or sounds outside your body and gently open your eyes.

Move your arms around and stretch your legs out, you may still feel a little befuddled and confused. Take a few moments to fully return into this world. Make yourself a cup of something, and step outside for fresh air. Let the feeling and emotions come and process them as you can. You may feel like a nap to clear your head. Do whatever feels right for you.

Hopefully, you found your calling place. If it's still uncertain, you can repeat this meditation as many times are you want to, and with luck it will come to you eventually. The key is perseverance – the journey will not always to be easy or straight forward, and these challenges are there to make finding the solution a truly enriching process.

I want to reassure you, sometimes you will find the unexpected answers in the places you least expect to find them. In your situation, the journey may be the most important part of the pilgrimage, and the destination simply the end of the journey. Or You might even come across the place that resonates for you on route to another destination all together.

My call to Iona was much later in my life than when Iona first started to manifest in my dreams, and I strongly believe that the calling will happen when it's meant to, for example, at a certain time in your life when its relevant and needed.

Chapter 7

Planning and Departure

Planning

You've decided to go on a pilgrimage, and you know where your destination is. The next step is to plan. I can't emphasise enough that it really pays to plan everything, you should plan everything, yes everything. From time off work, or away from your familiar life to how many ears plugs to take!

In 2017 I knew the time was right to start planning, but I was daunted because Iona is not an easy place to get to, especially from the other end of the UK, where I am based. As I don't drive, this meant the journey would involve planes, trains, buses, boats, and coaches, all of which had to be carefully orchestrated to meet each other or I would be stranded. Then there was the timescale to consider – how long would I stay on the island, (and where) and how many days should I allow to get here? I had other considerations too; my family, who I knew would be fully supportive, and my job, which gave me specific holiday dates, meaning I would be limited to times which were peak in the holiday seasons and therefore more expensive. This required that I have to carefully work out costs and budget to save enough, including working extra hours. But I felt compelled to overcome these obstacles and do what I could to go, so strong was the call of Iona on me.

The first things I had to consider were dates and where I would stay when I was there. As I mentioned in the last paragraph, due to my job I could only really take holiday during the school holidays. I didn't want to be visiting such a beautiful island in the winter, and summer holiday peak prices meant I had to go for early summer (summer term, half-term at the end of May) or autumn half term, (at the end of October). Unfortunately, either way it would only give me a total of seven days, so I would have to do careful planning of travel arrangements. I read information online, bought a travel guide to Iona, and searched accommodation websites. I had a checklist of things I wanted from the accommodation: my own room, so I could spend time, writing, reading, and sleeping without disruption, some food included would be good, distance from the harbour – somewhere easy to walk to at the end of a long journey. I had to be mindful of budget as well, which ruled out the hotels. I meticulously read reviews of each place, (I usually read customer reviews about everything, before I make a final decision on most things I buy, or places I stay,) weighing up the pros and cons. A couple of friends I knew online had recently made a trip to Iona, so I consulted them and got first-hand opinions too. In the end I chose a small family run bed and breakfast business, near to the harbour.

Travel was potentially going to be the biggest headache. With a limited timescale, I couldn't take a slow form, such as walking, (which at a rough estimate would take me 26 days if I walked eight hours a day, every day without fail.) The train from the south of England to the closest point of Oban involved around five changes, taking 22 hours each way, and was over £200 return. However, I could fly from my local airport to Glasgow in an hour and a half and it was cheaper than the train. I then would get a train from Glasgow to Oban, followed by a ferry to the Isle of Mull, which seemed to connect. Subsequently I would have to catch a bus across Mull to Fionnphort to take a short ferry journey across to Iona. This all seemed perfect on paper, a logistical dream, but I had a little trepidation – knowing the public transport system in the UK – and about how this would all work in practice. Nevertheless, I had to take a leap of faith and hope that it would all somehow work out... naive? Maybe....

A solid 18 hours (or near enough) of travelling. At the time I thought I must be a bit crazy!

I was lucky in that I planned my travel very carefully, but also that every aspect of the public transport I used, actually worked together that time. It could all have so easily gone wrong, and it's good to have a contingency plan if this proves necessary. Before you even consider the travel arrangements, you need to decide when you want to go and work out how long you can afford away from your everyday life. Perhaps you have limitations on when you can take leave? This in turn restricts the method of your journey. For instance, If you only have a week, then unless you live close to your place of calling, then walking, the most traditional form of pilgrimage, is impractical. If you have extended time away, such as a sabbatical of a few months, then walking would be a good (and cost effective,) choice. However, if you plan to walk you need to consider the weather and seasons before booking time off. You don't want to be walking through snow blizzards or the rainy season, but equally you don't want to be walking in 35-40 degrees heat.

The same goes for cycling, if you are planning to travel this way, then you will also need to check out roads and make sure you have an up-to-date road map of the area in which you are cycling. You will need to know how many miles or kg's you can travel on each day, and where you will sleep/eat or stay between your cycling. If you need to take a form of public transport, check out whether they accept bikes. Cycling will restrict the amount you can carry safely, meaning that you will have to consider each item's weight before you take it with you. I am thinking more specifically about a tent or similar here. For more on accommodation, please see later in the chapter.

Travelling by public transport, (by this I mean Bus, train, plane, coach, ferry etc.,) will need research, you may need to allow extra time between changes for lateness or distances between the various travel depots. It maybe that one aspect of the transport only leaves once a day or doesn't marry up with other parts of your travel plans, in which case, I would suggest looking at alternatives, for example, a taxi instead of a bus, if this is financially possible. Make sure when checking arranging your tickets you are aware if there is a difference between summer and winter timetables. If finances are important, then booking ahead is often a good way of getting the best price, though this does mean you are restricted to only catching that particular train/bus etc. Bear in mind that if you are travelling at peak times, then certain services might sell out if you don't book. I would advise doing research on each aspect of public transport – see what other travellers have said about the service – does it sell out? Is it reliable? Importantly, is it recommended?

Even after all your research, advance ticket buying and all the best planning in the world for public transport, it can still go wrong. Firstly, make sure you have a really good travel insurance that covers delays and cancellations. Secondly plan out what you would need to do in this situation – money for an extra night in a hotel, and new tickets for the next day, look at each point along your route and research all these options including where the tourist information centres (in the UK) are, who are very useful in an emergency.

The final form of travel I am including is driving a car or motorhome. This is, in my opinion, the most straight forward way of travelling and the easiest in terms of planning. Obviously if you are travelling to another country or continent, then you will also need to use public transport, such as a plane or boat, and will be restricted on the amount of luggage you can carry. If you are already starting in your own country, then you need to get from A to B. An essential purchase is an up-to-date road map and make sure you make allowances for finding petrol stations (In some places they are few and far between.) I would also recommend high quality vehicle insurance, especially if you are travelling long distances and you have little experience of driving in that country.

Then there's accommodation. There are multiple options here, starting with the most budget friendly: tents and wild camping, (though always check that it is permitted where you are pilgrimaging as it may not be permitted or be restricted to certain times of year). Your tent needs to be light and easy to assemble – you don't want to be stumbling around in the dark and pouring rain, trying to fix tent poles in the ground, similarly it needs to be small and light if you are carrying it. Another thing to consider if camping, is the peripheral items needed, such aa a stove, saucepan, sleeping bag, all of which need to be carried.

Hostels and bunkhouses are also a valid option on a budget. If you don't mind shared dormitories, (although there are an increasing number of single and even family rooms offered now a days) then you will have safety, a warm bed, the luxury of bathroom/kitchen facilities, and sometimes for an additional fee, breakfast. In the UK there are hostels in every area of the country, so they are a good option for walkers/cyclists and anyone who doesn't mind bunking up and being sociable. The other advantage is that, depending on the season, you might be able to simply turn up, especially on a rainy night when the tent doesn't hold the magical appeal it did a week ago.

Hotels and Bed and Breakfast accommodation are a great option if you want to have a little more luxury. You will have your own room and your own bathroom facilities and breakfast in the morning. The price range on hotels ranges from basic, to the top end which could include leisure facilities or spa experiences – although you might get raised eyebrows when you turn up in your muddy walking boots and wet rucksacks! With this section of accommodation, you will have plenty of choice, and can find one to fit your specific needs, much as I did on my pilgrimage to Iona.

If you are pilgrimaging on a well-known pilgrimage route, (such as the Camino de Santiago) then there may well be accommodation places specifically set up to cater for the pilgrim.

What you are going to take with you can be your next headache. If you are planning on being away for an extended period, especially if walking/cycling, then you need to make sure you have enough clothing but at the same time you also have a limit on how much you can carry. Can you washing at any of the places you are staying? If you are using a hotel or bed and breakfast, it may be possible to arrange to do some for a fee. It's definitely worth checking when booking. If you are camping, check out any towns or villages you pass through, as they may have a launderette. Make sure you have the right equipment for the environment you are travelling in, good walking boots, waterproof coat, and trousers, or lightweight but protective clothing and plenty of UPVC protection if it is hot. A quality bag or rucksack, which is waterproof and comfortable to wear for long periods of time, is essential. If camping, your tent needs to be lightweight and easy to carry, but also durable. Research absolutely everything!!

If you are flying you will have a weight and size limit, which means you might not be able to take everything with you. Can you do without certain things? Can you buy equipment or clothing when you get there?

Maps. Make sure you are familiar with the areas you are travelling through. Look for maps and do research to see how other pilgrims experienced the route you are taking if it's a known pilgrimage. If you have to navigate through an unpopulated area, then you will need a detailed map, and a compass, and I would recommend that you learn some practical navigation skills with an experienced outdoor teacher before you set off on your pilgrimage. Perhaps even have a trial run in an area near you at this essential skill before even starting to your pilgrimage.

Departure

Your physical departure at the beginning of your journey is the culmination of all your planning and preparations. I decided to share my own experience of literal departure and the journey to my destination, Iona. I hope this will give you understanding of this type of journey.

At last, the day arrived, and I got to the airport via taxi (no buses at that time of the morning). I have always been an early riser, so although I hadn't really slept the night before, I was wide awake before my alarm went off. I had packed, re-packed and checked everything at least a dozen times. I could only take cabin luggage, meaning everything had to cram into my rucksack, including my camera and walking stick (or pilgrim staff, if you prefer). I had been hoping and praying that all the elements would run smoothly, and the gods would be on my side that day. At the airport I found the arrivals/departure board and was relieved to see my flight was on time. The check-in was busy but straight forward, one of the rewards of a small airport. I sat in the departure lounge and re-examined my travel itinerary. A few days before I had created a wallet of notebook and tickets. In the notebook I had all the details of the travel companies, addresses, phone numbers, times, ticket numbers, prices, small maps if I needed to find something, and timetables in case things went awry. I also had a list of the addresses and phone numbers of tourist information places should I get really stuck and taxi companies as well as emergency bed and breakfasts. It had taken effort to create but I really recommend that you do this, it could save you a lot of fiddling around and time-consuming searching, not to mention panicking!

There was a two-and-a-half-hour gap between my flight landing and the train from Glasgow Queen Street to Oban, departing. In this time, I had to get a bus from the airport to the station. I figured it would also give me time to get lost, and then find my way again and eat something. The Airport Express buses are directly outside the main Glasgow airport terminal, and leave every ten minutes, 24 hours a day. I arrived at the entrance to Queen Street Station with an hour and a half to wait. Sitting in the station I did my usual people watching (a photographer's thing) and waiting for the announcement of what platform the train would come in on. The day had turned out to be warm and this was all the more pleasant because of the station's Victorian part-glass roof, meaning dappled sunshine gave the otherwise sterile station, a sense of airiness and warmth.

I had pre-booked my ticket, which had the advantage of reserving my seat, so I didn't have to stand all the way to Oban (three and a half hours.) I luckily had a window seat, and although the windows showed the signs of numerous journeys grime, I was treated to some spectacular views through the Trossachs National Park with views of Loch Lomond on the West Highland Line. My travelling companion was a fellow walker from Germany who was going to Mull. She happened to be knowledgeable about Iona and shared her maps and guidebooks of walks around the island. I was grateful to have someone who had caught the ferries and buses before to ensure that I was not going the wrong way with a bit of cheerful conversation to pass the time and relieve any stresses.

Arriving in Oban, I had been recommended by a friend that I should try scallops at a local fishing hut, but unfortunately the train was slightly late, and we had to hurry across the harbour to the ferry terminal to catch the ferry to Mull. Another friend had also been told me of a wonderful fish and chip cabin in

Fionnphort that served the best scallops, so was looking forward to a fish supper, later in the evening.

The Calmac company run the ferry routes in the Hebrides, and are very efficient, effortlessly managing what must have been a couple of hundred-foot passengers that afternoon. There is something I find very magical about traveling by sea to an island, especially one I have never visited before, it makes you almost feel like an explorer navigating the world in a ship – well Scotland anyway! This was a particularly beautiful sunny day, with the sapphire seas affording us the odd glimpse of a pod of porpoises and seals sunbathing on small rocky skerries between Mull and Oban harbour. Mull gradually became larger, and we disembarked at a brisk pace to get to the bus terminal at the end of the jetty.

The buses were actually more like coaches, which offered a higher level of comfort as we followed the single-track road away from Craignure to Fionnphort, a journey of an hour and a half – if there are no hold-ups. Luckily for me, it stated in various tourist guides that the Iona ferry waits for the bus. Interestingly, all the roads on Mull are single track, which appear to make every journey longer, although this is ideal for tourists as we glimpsed the glens and Ben More (The highest peak on Mull) and you do begin to appreciate a slower the pace of life, (and the remarkable skills of the bus drivers who have to navigate around broken-down tractors/camper vans with hair-raising sheer drops into the sea on the other sides, on a regular basis.)

When we finally arrived at Fionnphort, there was no time to check out the food or sights because the small Iona ferry was waiting to leave.

Chapter 8

Crossing the Threshold (and 'Thin' places)

What exactly does it mean to cross the threshold in a pilgrimage? Literally it means going from one place to another, a space between leaving and arriving, a liminal space or a moment of transition. In my journey to Iona, the threshold was crossing the sea, a natural physical boundary – and water is often considered a liminal threshold.

As it pulled out into the seas, I had an overpowering sense of déjà vu – that everything was familiar and I somehow recognised this sea, this voyage, this place – at the time I put this down to watching the Sacred Places of Britain programme a few years previously, as I mentioned earlier – but now I wonder if there was perhaps more to it. The view of Iona from the deck of the ferry – on a calm summer evening with a slight sea breeze and a note of salt in the air. The sun shone deeply onto the Abbey, which was a rich red colour contrasting with the teal sapphire of the calm waters and lush green of the land around it. Small white coloured houses were dotted here and there. Dun I, (the mountain,) loomed ever present behind, looking unusually peaceful and idyllic. I was completely overwhelmed with a lump in my throat and a tear in my eye. It seemed like I was becoming part of my own dream. I walked onto the jetty to the sound of sea birds and the gentle lapping of the sea. Iona was perfect.

On your pilgrimage, you will be crossing from the familiar into the unknown. Liminal space is one of the most important constituents of any spiritual quest or journey. It is here that we are challenged. Everything we are familiar with and our understanding of the everyday, the normal, collapses. We are now free to explore the unexplored and what exists beyond our normal human experiences and understanding. Here is liminal space.

You have experienced liminality before. Certain times of day are considered liminal, midday, for example, which is neither morning or afternoon, and midnight, which is between two days, or sometimes called betwixt. Twilight is another example of liminality, it is in a time between day and night, and this half-light can cause us to question what we perceive or see. Particular places are also liminal, and 'thin', for example, places that are thresholds between elements, such as bridges, which are neither on land, in the water or in the air, but somehow between all of them. A fairly common one is a doorway which is neither inside or out, a place betwixt and between. A river edge or shoreline, or even a cliff...all these places have a very particular feel, something different, indescribable and can offer a change in state of consciousness. Liminal spaces are passageways, they might help us connect one phase of our lives with another; for example, puberty which is between childhood and adulthood.

Exercise

Can you identify a liminal space near you in your local landscape? Visit one or some at one of the liminal times, such as midday or twilight. See if you can sense anything different there, a subtle change in atmosphere or energy, perhaps? Try closing your eyes and inhaling deeply, like in the meditative practices mentioned in pervious sections. Use your other senses, what can you hear, smell, or feel? The sensation of a difference may be very subtle.

Can you find the liminal spaces in your home? The borders or your property, the fences. Consider walking them (if you are able to) do they feel different than other areas? The entrance to your property is a particularly important threshold, can you sense this?

'Thin' places

Certain places, sometimes described as sacred or holy, can be 'thin' that is where the veil between this world and another – the Celtic Otherworld, the spiritual realm etc.' has been encountered and could be encountered today. These places could be anything, a building, a well, even an old oak or yew tree. or standing stones, for example.

Natural mounds and hillocks, old castles, ancient burial sites, misty hollows or lakes – these are the sort of places where the passing traveller might encounter the otherworld. But nowhere is more closely associated with its fantastic features than offshore islands. The risk of a sea passage adds a certain allure to anywhere across the water, while the coast itself tends to throw up its own visual ambiguities – refractive tricks of the light, land-like fog banks. Add to that the boundlessness of the ocean, the colourful tales of returning sailors, and it is no wonder that the western sea became such a bountiful playground of imaginary places.

Philip Marsden, *The Summer Isles.*

Iona is considered a thin place and I encountered it after my arrival and settling in, later that night. I decided to watch the sunset, so donning my boots and jacket, I headed north along the road as far as it went, and then along a track besides one of the small farms. I found the rocky beach and sat watching the sun set. My mind and thoughts lulled by the tide dragging in and out with stones, I was in that moment at one with this place of profound spirituality. It is said in Celtic myth that if you traverse the sea to an island, a passing traveller might encounter the Otherworld, a realm of the unknown, a place of shimmering wonder with golden magical beings, god-like and ethereal. Every aspect of the imagination could be fulfilled in the Otherworld, and I could feel how thin the veil between worlds was here. Time seemed to stand still and lost in my mediation with the land, I was stirred by the sudden cry of a gull overhead. I had sat on the stones for nearly three hours! I slept well that night.

Other places, as mentioned in the quote by Phillip Marsden, can be conduits to encounters with a different state of being, where the veil is thin, and you may well have had experience of this? Prior to considering any form of pilgrimage, I encountered a thin place when visiting Glastonbury Tor on a particularly foggy day. The top of the Tor seemed as if it were an island, almost floating in a sea of fog, with no other part of the surrounding landscape visible. It was disorientating and surreal. At times I felt as though if I took a step, I would be in an entirely different place.

Exercise

Maybe you are familiar with a place as mentioned above? If so, before embarking on your pilgrimage, make plans to visit. If you have never done this before, now is the time! Do an internet search or research such places in the library and make a point of visiting before your pilgrimage. Write about your experiences in your journal. How did you feel? Did you feel you were in a thin place and could easily step into another? Try drawing or sketching your experience.

Chapter 9

Arrival and Immersion

The next stage is reaching your destination and immersing yourself fully. You made it! Congratulations! All your hard work, your belief and your journey has led you to this point, your arrival!

From my own experience, I know that precious moment is magical. I remember stepping from the boat onto the slipway, the water lapping around my boots. I resisted the urge to remove them and walk barefoot as I was finally there. I felt my eyes prickle with tears.

To the people who live on Iona, every ferry that arrives in the summer months, brings thousands of visitors – tourists and pilgrims alike. Every visitor is treated with respect and courtesy, but also nonchalance. This suited me, as I breathed in the clean air and admired the white beach beside the slip way, all the while, trying to contain the differing emotions that nearly overcame me. I wanted to cry my eyes out and at the same time, whoop with joy. I had arrived!

I walked as though on air, down to the main road which ran from the slip way and is the only road on the island. I followed the crowd ahead of me as we meandered around the concentration of houses on the island, my head was still in the clouds, my heart unable to fully grasp that I was finally here. As we all turned the next corner, I saw the Abbey and the sea overlooking Mull, It was as if I was in my childhood dreams, seeing the sapphire blue sea and rich green of the land, the Abbey striking in the warming evening sunshine.

There is nothing that can truly express this feeling, the closest I can come to is deep serenity. My heart was in the landscape, my mind sailed around with the clouds and wind overhead!

Eventually I refocused my mind by searching for the bed and breakfast house I was staying in. The owner was a native islander and able to lend her years of wisdom to my plans for the next few days. She was able to advice on cafes, walking routes, the best time to visit the Abbey (for free at the daily service at 9pm,) and even the best spots to try and see the recently sited pod of porpoises from the shore. Finding a good place to stay had been one of my top priorities when initially planning my pilgrimage.

After I had freshened up, I decided to walk to the end of the island (Iona is only just over three miles long,) the sun was just beginning to set, and I was treated to a hue of golden light hitting the rocks and see, with only myself for company. As I stood looking out from the rocks on the beach, felt as though I had reached the end of the world and could almost touch another, more sacred, unseen one. All around me I felt the presence of the land and its power.

I closed my eyes and sat in harmony with the world, I breathed the land in and was completely aware of at one with it. It Is probably one of the most powerful experiences of my life.

In thin places, time tends to play tricks, and before I knew it, hours had passed in what seemed to be minutes. I returned to my bed and slept well, all the while I heard the land calling through the wind blowing against my window.

The next day, I made my way down to St Columba's Bay at the opposite end of the island. I decided that when I had passed the residential area, when the roads slipped away becoming beach then common land, I would walk bare foot to the bay. I have always been a person who prefers to have nothing on her feet, and although areas were harder to walk, with care and mindfulness, it became easier to overcome the small level

of discomfort. The connection I felt with the land was only heightened. The land itself is a mixture of different landscapes, from bog and rough grasses to rocks and sand, which I found added to the sensory experience of walking barefoot.

As I climbed down the last rocky area, I was treated to a vista of the bay, sheep, and sapphire oceans. It was breath-taking!

Upon the area before the beach, a labyrinth is set out with stones in a simply Troy-town style. Beside this, a St Brigid's Cross. I decided to walk the labyrinth and closed my eyes feeling my way with my feet on the stones. My mind was clear as I listened to the calls of gulls overheard, the baaing of sheep and the wind whipping in the grasses. As I have already said, time moves differently in thin places, and as I slowed my breath, I could feel the land and energies surrounding me. The labyrinth path became my journey to reach Iona, every step one part of the path to this place. At the centre I became one with the spirit of the land, every gull, every sheep. Every blade of grass swaying

in the wind, and every wave against the shore. I felt immense in power and minute in physicality.

I sat myself on a large stone beside the shoreline. The sun was now strong as the day headed to its middle, and I enjoyed the warmth. My attention was grabbed by two fellow visitors to the bay, laughing together and crunching across the stones towards the water's edge. They immediately stripped and dashed into the water, squealing at the temperature! I decided that a dip wouldn't go amiss but my modesty made me wait until the couple had left the immediate area.

The water was indeed cold, but also exhilarating and overcoming the initial shock I lay upon my back and watched the blue sky overhead. I stayed in for five minutes and then returned to my rock to dry in the sun, which was blessedly still warm. I tasted the salt on my lips and sipped water. I considered this area of land. St Columba landed here, it was the first place from where he saw Iona, and I wondered what had gone through his mind as he and his disciples pulled their coracle up onto the beach. Had he stopped to taste the salt on his lips, like me? Had the day been sunny and the land, therefore attractive, or had it been stormy and rugged?

After I dressed, I decided to look for Iona marble or green stone. This was harder than you'd think to find but I count myself lucky to have found a couple of small pieces to meditate with now. Many years ago, there was a fully commercial mine on the island to extract the marble/greenstone to make jewellery and export. This seems to have been a flash in the pan venture, but Iona greenstone is still used in jewellery and sought after today.

Later as I walked back towards the town area, enjoying the sand beneath my feet, I thought of Robert Louis Stevenson who had visited Iona and stayed at one of the hotels. Later he used the island of Erraid (South of Iona) in his famous novel *Kidnapped*. David Balfour, the hero, is marooned there, existing on limpets and bog water. I tried to imagine being marooned on an island of granite boulders in rainstorms with no shelter, an inhospitable place of danger. Balfour found comfort from his misery by looking towards Iona *"I could catch sight of the great ancient church and the roofs of people's houses in Iona."* He would see the smoke rising in the morning and evening. *"I used to watch this smoke, when I was wet and cold, and my head half turned with loneliness; and think of the fireside and company til my heart burned."* The idea that Iona brought hope and warmth into the heart of someone so lost, in turn gave me a deeper understanding about the power of belief and its strength in someone's soul.

I visited the Heritage Centre back towards the town later in the day and enjoyed studying photos and learning about the history of the island from the last couple of centuries. I found a small, charming book *Flowers of Iona* by Jean M. Millar and published by Isle of Iona Press. This book has proved so popular that it has been reprinted and revised three times since originally coming out in 1972. As you have guessed, the book is indeed about flowers but also gives a fascinating overview of many other wild plants found here. I eagerly read it while sitting in the garden of the little café next door, and as I walked back to my lodgings, mindfully along the lanes, I immediately spotted several flowers featured, including dog violets and early purple orchids, so small that I imagine most visitors would not really notice. This small gesture of understanding filled my heart with satisfaction, and I determined to seek out other small glimpses of hidden beauty.

I visited the Abbey the next morning, which is at the heart of the community on Iona. Cared for by Historic Scotland, its decorations and offerings are tangible, simple everyday gifts from the land, along with candles and symbols of the faith. I found this simplicity very moving and human. The interior when I visited, was lit by natural light, often shafts of sunlight falling in significant places, along walls and signs of faith. The tenderness and care offered by the community to this small Abbey is emotive. The power of belief palpable, striking and I couldn't help but be moved to tears as I lit a candle for a departed loved one.

To the side of the Abbey is St Odhran's Chapel, (St Oran) which is free to visit and always open. This again is simplistic with wooden benches and humble decoration. St Odhran was one of Columba's twelve missionaries that accompanied him from Ireland. Legend says that the original church Columba and his companions built kept falling down and so Columba had a vision that one of his faithful would have to be sacrificed in order for the church to stand. William Sharp, writing as Fiona Macdonald tells the tale in 1900:

Colum Cille said to his people: 'It is well for us that our roots should go underground here;' and he said to them, 'It is permitted to you that some one of you go under the earth of this island to consecrate it.' Odran rose up readily, and thus he said: 'If thou wouldst accept me,' he said, "I am ready for that.'...Odran then went to heaven.

He was buried alive, and the building stood.

Today St Odhran's Chapel is the oldest structure standing on Iona, built in the 12th century, and is built on an even older wooden structure. The building ley derelict for years until it was restored along with the Abbey in the 1900s. Surrounding the chapel are the graves of many including most recently John Smith of the Labour party who sadly died in the 1994. Relleig Odhran has been used as a burial place since the time of Columba and a survey conducted in 1549 listed 48 Dalradian/Scottish kings buried here, as well as eight Norwegian and four Irish kings.

Sitting inside the chapel I felt a deep connection with the past and felt a real sense of the divine around me. I decided to return the next morning when it would be quieter before visitors to the island arrived and try to commune with the spirit of the place.

I have not mentioned before, the reason for my visit to Iona at this particular time in my life, (admittedly I did hint that the time had to be right in the introduction). In the six months prior to coming to Iona I had been diagnosed with a life-threatening brain tumour, moreover it has directly behind my left eye and there was a danger of imminent blindness unless operated on soon. The operation would involve replacing a significant portion of my skull and the whole orbital area with an artificial implant as the tumour had ravaged this section of my skull. The operation was happening a few days after I returned from Iona. On the one hand I was relieved that the tumour would be removed, and I would not go blind. However, because of the length of surgery, there was still a chance I would not wake up.

Until I was sitting in this tiny chapel on Iona, I believed that I had resigned myself to my fate and accepted all outcomes. As I sat in the coolness of semi-light the next morning – my last on Iona, I allowed myself to cry and ask for, well, I don't know exactly – I just wanted to share my anguish and be heard by something or someone else. I felt genuinely that the divinity, as I called it, in this place was compassionate and would understand.

Let me point out, here and now, that the following may sound perhaps crazy and I agree. I have laid it out for your perusal, your contemplation and, of course, you are free to come to your own conclusions.

To my utter surprise, when I stopped crying, before me was a figure, not solid and definitely not of this world. I could not tell by sight whether it was male or female, until I heard in my mind what was conveyed in a series of words and images. I thought I was dreaming and rubbed my eyes and stood up, stamping my feet to wake myself. He told me that I was never alone, that whatever happened – if I lived or didn't, I would be held, and that the divine was always with me. I pointed out that I was not a Christian and that I was also a woman. He said that was irrelevant, the divine one that he spoke of was of all faiths and no faith and was the creator of everything. This divine one was so ancient, far beyond comprehension and yet newborn every day with the dawn. This divine one was genderless and besides, he pointed out, that there were women in the Abbey and chapels, and the idea of it being all men at his time, was a modern fallacy. The figure then laid his hands on my shoulders and told me again that I was not alone and was always held...

At that moment, the caretaker opened the door of the chapel, which creaked loudly echoing in the tiny space and I turned around in surprise and shock. He looked in, saw me, and apologetically withdrew. The figure and vision before me had vanished. I sat again trying to comprehend what had just happened. I was completely shocked, overwhelmed, and light-headed. I was totally convinced I was deluded. I have no idea how long I sat there unable to move and unable to stop crying. After a time, a white feather floated down in front of me and landed at my feet. I looked around, for a bird or someone there, but it was just me and everything was silent.

When I was ready, I picked up the feather and lit a candle beside the altar. I thanked St Odhran for his kindness and words of comfort. As an afterthought, I wrote a prayer request which I placed in the basket. I walked out of the chapel into the most beautiful sunshine and looked at the horizon remembering that this divine being, this god, Odhran had told me of, was re-born every dawn. I walked towards the ferry slipway but on second thoughts, walked past towards the white sands next to it. I slipped off my shoes and stood exalted in the cold azure blue waters of this most remarkable place for the last time. I wanted to drink in every feeling, every sight, every smell, and sound. I wanted this place to be imprinted on me, forever.

I knew that whether alive or not, I would return here to my heart place, in some way.

Chapter 10

Going Home

So, you have returned from your pilgrimage to your regular life. In some ways this may seem to be the hardest aspect. Pilgrimage will have changed you. This could be in a small way, for example, your fitness level has improved, or it may be significant. Pilgrimage may make you question everything in your life, your understanding of the world and your place in it.

As mentioned in the previous chapter, almost immediately after I returned from my pilgrimage, I underwent major surgery,. The immediacy of my own change from pilgrimage was that I wasn't afraid. I had been given the gift of companionship in either death or life and I would be supported spiritually. This comfort was deeply meaningful to me and allowed me to be strong in both my preparations before the surgery and during my recovery.

Although I am not a believer in the Christian god, or any form of Christian dogma, I do, now believe I had what would have been called a vision. Whether this vision was entirely in my mind, or actually happened, I cannot say and I am sure lots of people will have theories relating to this. What I do know if that I was given a tremendous gift: trust in the divine.

In the weeks and months after my return, I grew in confidence and was no longer afraid of what life would throw at me. I believe that my survival was because of my internal strength, which in turn was given by powers beyond myself. Since my return I have always strived to take notice of coincidences and my intuition when things happen in a pattern, or give me a strong sensation that I should be aware of them. I often take meaning from the small, everyday things and I endeavour to help others do the same.

My advice to you, after your return and reintegration into your life, would be to take time to adjust back if you are able to. Spend time evaluating your journey to this point. Consider meditating or journeying and look at what you achieved in your pilgrimage. Has your personal philosophy changed or been strengthened? Do you see things in a different way now? If you are unsure, take a look at your journal and re-read your notes.

After a time, journey in meditation back to the sacred place. Take note of your emotions and feelings as you visit spiritually; how do you feel now, after a period of time has passed? Have your thoughts changed at all? Importantly, keep journalling, create artwork, or even sing about your experience in pilgrimage if this helps.

Do you now have a clear goal, or purpose in your life? This may simply be to be more present, be more understanding of others, it maybe that you wish to dedicate yourself to a deity or spiritual lifestyle. You might now wish to study intensely and become a student, for example.

It could be that you want to change your life completely. You may decide that you wish to move to the other side of the world, or change careers, or leave your current situation? It could be that you don't change anything in your life, except your attitude, or it might be that the values you built your existence on have shifted in one way or another.

In a way, you could say, you have been reborn into a new perspective. You are looking through new eyes at a new world, at least to you. It also may be the case that you want to go on more pilgrimages to new places and find more meaning and fulfilment in the very act of being a pilgrim.

Whatever way it is for you, I wish you all the luck in the world.

Epilogue

A Final Pilgrimage

In 2023 I finally got to do a short pilgrimage to visit St. Wite's Shrine in Dorset. I had read much about her shrine and its importance as a pilgrimage site from the time of Alfred The Great. The Shrine of St Wite is one of only two remaining original shrines in the UK, the other is Edward The Confessor's shrine in St. Paul's Cathedral, London.

Little is known about St. Wite, she was quite small in height and around 40 years old when she died, according to records made when examining her remains. There are lots of Christians theories about exactly who she was, and the church renamed her Candida, (Meaning white) though her original name is still more commonly used. A strong tradition locally is that she was a Saxon holy woman who was martyred during a Danish raid nearby in the ninth century. In the church itself there are some old carvings of a Viking ship in the church tower.

Alfred the Great himself had St Wite's church erected fifty years later, and regularly visited the church on pilgrimage. During the height of pilgrimage, the church was one of the most popular, along with St Wites Well in nearby Morcombelake. She is remembered as a healer of the sick, and even today there are dozens of prayer cards placed in her shrine, asking for healing.

I had wanted to finish this book with a pilgrimage, and as covid dragged on, the church was closed throughout 2020 and 2021 and with severely limited opening times until the end of 2022, making a visit seemingly impossible with work and family commitments increasing.

By chance, earlier this month I finally had the opportunity. I set off from Stonebarrow Hill, near Bridport in Dorset, with its spectacular views over the sea and Jurassic coastline and walked part of the South Coast Path. I climbed slowly to the famous Golden Cap which is the highest point on the coastline. Although the day was quite grey, I had stunning views – this alone was worth the walk! As I turned away from the coastline, I walked along hedgerow-lined paths towards the ruins of St. Gabriel's Chapel. This was a pleasant place to pause and enjoy the peace and quiet. The church fell into disrepair during the 19th century and now is open for visitors to enjoy a resting place. The path became narrower as I came to St Wites Well. The well is very unassuming but nicely preserved. I paused again and sampled the water. I was pleased to see that it was clear of ritual rubbish.

From here it is signposted to the Canonicorum and a pleasant stroll downhill. The sleepy village is as ancient as the origins of the church. The original Saxon church is gone, except the shrine, and the current one dates form the 12th century. Surrounding the church are yews, which, to me, indicates an older, pre-Saxon site that is lost, however, there is no evidence of this.

St Wite's shrine is fairly plain, made of Purbeck marble and local Golden stone, with St. Wite's remains housed within a lead casket. It is against the North wall and has three oval openings in which prayers are placed, or preying hands placed within. On the floor in front are cushions to kneel upon. Near to this are chairs to sit upon. I am not of the Christian faith but always feel a deep sense of reverence and the power of belief that must have filled the hearts of all who have visited this ancient place.

I lit a candle and asked for healing on a prayer card for the world, which in a way, felt strange as I was in a such small village in front of a shrine that had remained here for over 1,200 years. The beauty of it was the simplicity of devotion and I could appreciate the power of faith. I was thankful that St. Wite's shrine still exists in this quiet part of the UK.

As I left and headed towards the path, I knew that it would be a place of returning one day. It was privilege and very much worth the wait!

Bibliography

Anderson, Andrew. *The Ritual of Writing.* (2019) Moon Books.

Artress, Lauren. *Walking a Spiral Path.* (2006) Riverhead Books.

Asser, John. *Alfred the Great, Asser's Life of King Alfred and Other Contemporary Sources.* (1983) Penguin.

Bentley, Jane & Paynter, Neil. *Around A Thin Place. An Iona Pilgrimage Guide.* (2011) Wild Goose Publications.

Bowden-Pickstock, Susan. Quiet Gardens, *Roots of Faith?* (2009) Bloomsbury.

Calder, Jenni. *RLS A Life Study.* (1980) Hamish Hamilton.

Chatwin, Brue. *The Songlines.* (1998) Vintage Classics.

Chaucer, Geoffrey. *The Canterbury Tales.* (2005 ed.) Penguin.

Clubley, Richard. *Orkney. A Special Place.* (2017) Luath press.

Coelho, Paulo. *The Pilgrimage.* (1997) Thorsons.

Conze, Edward. *Buddhism: A Short History.* (2008) Oxford University Press.

Dell, Christopher. *Mythology, The Complete Guide to Our Imagined Worlds.* (2012) Thames and Hudson.

Dillon, Matthew. *Pilgrims and Pilgrimage in Ancient Greece.* (1997) Psychology Press.

Dirdan-Smith, Jo. *The Essance of Buddhism.* (2016) Arcturus

Forest, Danu. *Gwyn ap Nudd: Wild god of Faery, Guardian of Annwfn.* (2017) Moon Books.

Gogerty, Clare. *Beyond The Footpath.* (2019) Piatkus.

Herman, AL. *Hinduism: A Brief Introduction.* (1991) Westview.

Higgins, Charlotte. *Red Thread.* (2018) Vintage.

Hoffman, CM. *Judaism: An Introduction.* (2010) London Press.

Hutton, Ronald. *Pagan Britian.* (2013) Yale University Press.

Hyland, Angus & Wilson, Kendra. *The Maze – A Labyrinthine Compendium.* (2018) Laurence King Publishing.

Ivakhiv, Adrian. Claiming *Sacred Ground. Pilgrims and Politics at Glastonbury and Sedona.* (2001) Indiana University Press.

Jones, Kathy. *In the Nature of Avalon.* (2000) Ariadne Publications.

Lonegren, Sig. *Labyrinths -Ancient Myths and Modern Uses.* (2007) Gothic Image Publications.

Marsden, Philip. *The Summer Isles.* (2019) Granta.

May, Katherine. *The Electricity of Every Living Thing.* (2019) Trapeze.

Nesbitt, Eleanor. *Sikhism: A Short Introduction.* (2016) Oxford University Press.

Pinch, Geraldine. *Egyptian Mythology: A Guide to the Gods, Goddesses, and Traditions of Ancient Egypt.* (2004) Oxford University Press.

Porter, Venetia. *Hajj: Journey to the Heart of Islam.* (2012) British Museum.

Reader, Ian. *A Simple Guide to Shinto.* (1998) Global.

Rufin, Jean-Christophe. *The Santiago Pilgrimage.* (2013) Maclehose Press.

Rumble, Alexander. *The Reign of Cnut: King of England/Denmark.* (1999) Leicester University Press.

Shapland, Andrew. *Labyrinth: Knossos, Myth and Reality.* (2023) Ashmolean Museum.

Simpson, Liz. *The magic of Labyrinths.* (2003) Element.

Stevenson, Robert Louis. *Kidnapped.* (1925) Tusitala Edition. Chatto and Windus.

Stevenson, Robert Louis. *Travels With a Donkey.* (1925) Tusitala Edition. Chatto and Windus.

Sugden, Keith. *Walking The Pilgrim Ways.* (1991) David & Charles.

Symington, Martin. *Britian's Sacred Places.* (2022) Bradt.

Tharoor, Shashi. Why I am a Hindu. (2021) Hurst & Company, London.

Thompson, Claire. Mindfulness & The natural World. (2013) Leaping Hare Press.

Ure, John. Pilgrimage. (2006) Constable. London.

Webb, Diana. Pilgrimage in Medieval England. (2000) Carnegie Publishing.

Waters, Christine. Who was St. Wite? (1980) Whitchurch Canonicorum.

Winn, Raynor. The Salt Path. (2018) Penguin.

Woodsford-Dean, Helen & Mark. This Old Golden Land. (2020) Spiritual Orkney.

Articles and Chapters

Balch, Oliver & McCulloch, Adam. *20 Superb UK Walks for Families, Day-trippers and Long-Distance Rambles.* (23/4/16) The Guardian Newspaper.

Bowmen, Marion. *Going With the Flow. Contemporary Pilgrimage in Glastonbury.* p. 241 – 280. In Ed. Margry, Peter-Jan. *Shrines of Pilgrimage in the Modern World.* (2008). Amsterdam University Press.

Bowman, Marion. *Procession and Possession in Glastonbury: Continuality of Change and the Manipulation of Tradition.* (2004) from Folklore Vol.115. No3 (December 2004) Taylor and Francis Ltd. JSTOR https://www.jstor.org/stable/30035212Balch,

Butterfield, Fox. *China's Majestic Huangshan.* (2/8/81) New York Times Online.

Wills, Dixe. *And Did Those Feet...15 Pilgrim Trails in the UK & Europe.* (2/11/19) The Guardian newspaper.

Author Solves Dunning Witch Mystery (24/6/11) The Daily Record Online.

Websites (Not given in the main body of the book)

Abydos, Ancient Egypt: https://www.britannica.com/place/Abydos-ancient-city-Egypt (Last accessed 19/08/23)

Graceland: https://www.graceland.com/ (Last accessed 20/03/20)

Jarrow March: https://www.bbc.co.uk/history/british/britain_wwone/jarrow_01.shtml (Last accessed 07/04/20)

Mindfulness: https://www.mind.org.uk/information-support/drugs-and-treatments/mindfulness/mindfulness-exercises-tips/ (Last accessed 23/08/23)

Peace Pilgrim: https://www.peacepilgrim.org/ (Last accessed 07/04/20)

The Walsingham Way: https://www.walsingham.org.uk/the-walsingham-way/ (Last accessed 17/09/22)

MOON BOOKS
PAGANISM & SHAMANISM

What is Paganism? A religion, a spirituality, an alternative
belief system, nature worship? You can find support for
all these definitions (and many more) in dictionaries,
encyclopaedias, and text books of religion, but subscribe to
any one and the truth will evade you. Above all Paganism is
a creative pursuit, an encounter with reality, an exploration
of meaning and an expression of the soul. Druids, Heathens,
Wiccans and others, all contribute their insights and literary
riches to the Pagan tradition. Moon Books invites you
to begin or to deepen your own encounter,
right here, right now.

If you have enjoyed this book, why not tell other readers by
posting a review on your preferred book site.

Readers of ebooks can buy or view any of these bestsellers by clicking on the live link in the title. Most titles are published in paperback and as an ebook. Paperbacks are available in traditional bookshops. Both print and ebook formats are available online.

Find more titles and sign up to our readers' newsletter
www.collectiveinkbooks.com/paganism

For video content, author interviews and more, please subscribe to our YouTube channel.

MoonBooksPublishing

Follow us on social media for book news, promotions and more:

Facebook: Moon Books

Instagram: @MoonBooksCI

X: @MoonBooksCI

TikTok: @MoonBooksCI